BARNDOMINIUM LIVING MADE SIMPLE

SIMPLIFIED STRATEGIES FOR BUILDING AND THRIVING IN YOUR RUSTIC MODERN DREAM HOME

BO MURPHY

CONTENTS

Introduction — 5

1. Laying the Foundation — 9
   Understanding Barndominiums
2. Planning Your Project — 25
   From Vision to Blueprint
3. Navigating Permits and Regulations — 37
4. Building Your Team — 51
   Contractors and DIY Approaches
5. Construction Phase — 65
   From Groundbreaking to Finish
6. Design and Decor — 77
   Creating Your Unique Space
7. Settling In — 89
   Transitioning to Barndominium Living
8. Realizing the Dream — 101
   Success Stories and Future Trends

Conclusion — 115
References — 119

INTRODUCTION

A family from the bustling suburbs made a bold change not long ago. They sought a home that offered more than just shelter—a place where they could connect, create, and thrive. They stumbled upon the idea of a barndominium. A year later, they found themselves in a space that was not only functional but full of character. Their barndominium combined rustic charm with modern comfort, allowing them to live on their own terms. This transformation is not just a story of building a house; it's about creating a lifestyle.

But what exactly is a barndominium? Originally, it was a simple idea—a barn converted into a living space. Over time, it has become a popular housing choice, unification the best of both worlds. Barndominiums offer the wide-open spaces of barns with the comforts of modern homes. They're versatile, affordable, and customizable. In recent years, they've gained nationwide traction, appealing to those who value form and function.

This book is your guide to understanding and creating your own barndominium. It will help you navigate the practical challenges of estimating costs, managing construction timelines, and finding the right balance between design and functionality. It will also support you through the emotional journey of transitioning to this unique lifestyle. From planning to living, this book covers it all.

If you're new to the concept of barndominiums, you're not alone. This book is tailored for those who are ready to explore this innovative housing option. Many are drawn to barndominiums for their affordability and the chance to personalize every aspect. Others are motivated by a desire for sustainable living. Whatever your reason, this book speaks to your aspirations.

There are many benefits to living in a barndominium. Compared to traditional housing, you can save money. You have the freedom to design a space that truly suits your needs. You can simplify your life, focusing on what matters most. Imagine crafting a home that reflects your unique style, where every corner tells a story. That's the potential of a barndominium.

Yet, with any new venture come concerns. Some worry about durability or the aesthetic appeal of a barndominium. These concerns are valid, but fear not. Throughout this book, you'll find solutions and reassurances. You'll learn how to build a barndominium that's not only sturdy but also beautiful.

The chapters ahead will guide you through the process step by step. We'll start with planning and construction, move into design and customization, and finally, discuss lifestyle adaptation and future growth. Each chapter builds on the last, ensuring you have a clear path forward.

The goal of this book is simple. By the end, you'll have practical, actionable insights to help you successfully build and live in your own barndominium. You'll gain the confidence and knowledge needed to turn your vision into reality.

On a personal note, my passion lies in helping beginners like you overcome challenges. I believe that everyone deserves to achieve their dream lifestyle. Over the years, I've seen the joy and fulfillment that comes from creating a home that truly fits one's life. I'm dedicated to providing reputable, easy-to-follow guidance.

As you embark on this journey, please keep an open mind. Consider the possibilities that lie before you. Envision your dream home and the life you want to lead. This book is here to inspire and support you every step of the way.

Welcome to the world of barndominium living. Let's get started.

CHAPTER ONE

LAYING THE FOUNDATION
UNDERSTANDING BARNDOMINIUMS

When you hear the term "barndominium," what comes to mind? For many, it's the image of a traditional barn transformed into a cozy, modern home. This concept isn't just a trend; it's a movement toward a lifestyle that balances simplicity with innovation. Imagine stepping into a space that once housed hay or livestock, now converted into a warm, inviting home with all the comforts you desire. The charm of a barndominium is not just in its unique aesthetic but also in its ability to adapt to the needs of those who inhabit it. As you explore this chapter, you'll uncover the roots and evolution of barndominiums, gaining insight into why they've captured the imagination of so many.

1.1 WHAT IS A BARNDOMINIUM? EXPLORING THE BASICS

A barndominium is more than just a fancy name for a barn conversion. At its core, it's a concept that marries rustic elements with modern living. The idea first gained popularity in the late 1980s when people began to see the potential of transforming unused barns into homes. These structures offered large open spaces, high ceilings, and a structural integrity that was ideal for residential use. Over time, the term "barndominium" has expanded to encompass a range of styles, from the traditional wooden frame to modern steel constructions. These homes retain the distinctive barn shape, often featuring sloped roofs and expansive sliding doors, but inside, they boast all the amenities of a contemporary dwelling.

The origins of barndominiums can be traced back to agricultural buildings that have existed for centuries, serving as functional spaces for farming needs. Historically, barns were designed to withstand harsh weather and provide ample storage for equipment and crops. This durability and practicality have carried over into their modern adaptations. As people began to see the potential in these robust structures, a new way of living emerged, one that combined the best features of traditional barns with the comforts of a modern home. The evolution of barndominiums is a testament to human ingenuity and the desire to create spaces that cater to both utility and comfort.

The structural elements of a barndominium are key to its appeal. Typically, these homes use metal framing and siding, which offer superior strength and durability compared to conventional wood framing. This choice of materials not only contributes to the longevity of the building but also provides a sleek, industrial aesthetic that many find appealing. Open floor plans are another hallmark of barndominium design. With minimal interior walls, these spaces feel expansive and airy, allowing for a seamless flow between different areas of the home. Insulated panels are often used to enhance energy efficiency, helping maintain a comfortable indoor climate year-round.

Barndominiums are versatile in their use, extending beyond traditional residential purposes. Many owners appreciate the ability to integrate workspaces, such as home offices, studios, or workshops, directly into their living environment. This flexibility particularly appeals to those who work remotely or pursue creative endeavors. Additionally, the open layouts and high ceilings provide ample space for storage, accommodating everything from vehicles to recreational equipment. For some, a barndominium serves a dual purpose: a home and a commercial space. This adaptability makes barndominiums an attractive option for a wide variety of lifestyles.

In recent years, barndominiums have gained popularity across diverse demographics. One reason is their cost-effectiveness. Compared to traditional homes, barndominiums often require less initial construction and ongoing maintenance investment. This affordability and the potential for customization attract many first-time homebuyers and those looking to downsize. The flexibility in design allows owners to create spaces that reflect their personal style and meet their unique needs. For those seeking a rural or semi-rural lifestyle, barndominiums offer an appealing combination of modern convenience and pastoral charm, providing a perfect retreat from the hustle and bustle of city life.

1.2 THE APPEAL OF BARNDOMINIUMS: AFFORDABILITY AND FLEXIBILITY

Barndominiums present a remarkable opportunity for those seeking a home that doesn't break the bank. Traditional homes often entail a significant financial burden, but barndominiums offer a more budget-friendly alternative. Their simpler designs lead to lower construction costs, a factor that cannot be overstated in today's economic climate. The expenses typically associated with building a home are drastically reduced by utilizing straightforward structures and materials. This affordability is further accentuated by the potential for do-it-yourself building approaches, allowing homeowners to save on labor costs. Those with a knack for building can contribute their skills, transforming their barndominium without the hefty price tag of hiring a full crew. Moreover, maintenance expenses are notably lower, largely due to the durability of materials like metal framing, which require less upkeep than traditional wooden structures.

Flexibility in design is another compelling advantage of barndominiums. Unlike conventional homes, where altering the layout can be daunting, barndominiums offer the freedom to easily modify floor plans. This adaptability is a boon for those who wish to incorporate personal touches and features. Whether you dream of a spacious open-plan living area or a more segmented design to accommodate various needs, a barndominium can adapt to your vision. The modular nature of these homes also means that expansion is a feasible option. As your needs evolve, your home can grow with you through additional rooms or expanded living spaces. This flexibility caters to personal preferences and ensures that your home remains functional and relevant over time.

The potential for multi-use spaces in a barndominium is another aspect that sets it apart. These homes are not just about living; they are about living well and making the most of available space. Imagine a home where your living room effortlessly transforms into a workspace or a guest room doubles as a home office. This versatility is particularly appealing in today's world, where remote work and multifunctional spaces are increasingly valued. Barndominiums can accommodate recreational areas alongside residential zones, providing room for hobbies, workouts, or relaxation without compromising the living space. This adaptability extends to the outdoors, where expansive surroundings offer opportunities for gardens, workshops, or even small-scale agriculture, mixing lifestyle and functionality seamlessly.

Beyond the structural and financial advantages, barndominiums offer lifestyle benefits that contribute to a simpler, more fulfilling way of life. Living in a barndominium often means residing in rural or semi-rural areas, which fosters a deeper connection to nature. This proximity to the natural world encourages activities like gardening, promoting self-sufficiency and providing immense satisfaction and peace. The opportunity to cultivate your own food and live sustainably is a significant draw for many, offering a rewarding and environmentally friendly lifestyle. Additionally, barndominiums in less populated areas facilitate community-building, allowing for close-knit relationships with neighbors and a sense of belonging that is often absent in urban settings. This sense of community enhances the quality of life, providing a supportive network that enriches everyday experiences.

In essence, barndominiums provide an accessible entry point into homeownership with the added benefits of customization and a lifestyle emphasizing sustainability and community. These homes are more than just a place to live; they are a canvas for creativity, a haven for personal growth, and a gateway to a life that values simplicity and connection above all else.

1.3 LIFESTYLE SHIFT: EMBRACING RURAL AND SEMI-RURAL LIVING

Transitioning to rural or semi-rural living is not just about changing your address; it requires a shift in mindset and daily habits. The pace of life is noticeably slower, offering a stark contrast to the hustle and bustle of city living. This change is invigorating for some, providing a sense of peace and room to breathe. It allows time for reflection and a chance to truly appreciate simpler things. You find yourself waking to the sounds of nature rather than the blare of traffic. Time stretches, giving you the opportunity to savor moments that might have been hurried through before. Adjusting to this slower rhythm might take time, but it offers a rewarding experience of living more intentionally.

Embracing self-sufficiency is another key aspect of rural living. With more space and fewer conveniences at your doorstep, you might find yourself drawn to DIY projects or learning new skills. This is an opportunity to grow, whether it's planting a garden, building a piece of furniture, or tackling home repairs. The satisfaction of completing a project with your own hands is unparalleled. It fosters a sense of independence and accomplishment. These skills become invaluable in the countryside, where resources aren't always readily available. You learn to rely on your ingenuity and creativity, turning challenges into opportunities.

Living away from urban centers comes with myriad benefits, including increased privacy and space. Your home is not just a place to sleep but a sanctuary away from the prying eyes and noise of city life. Imagine looking out your window and seeing only nature, with no buildings obstructing your view. Your nearest neighbor might be a mile away, giving you the freedom to live without constraint. This privacy is a luxury that urban dwellers often yearn for. The ample space surrounding you also means more room for hobbies or outdoor activities, whether creating a workshop or starting a farm.

One of the most profound advantages of rural living is a closer connection with nature. You're no longer removed from the natural world; you're surrounded by it daily. Fresh air, open fields, and star-filled nights become your norm. This connection can ground you, providing a sense of belonging to something larger. It encourages a lifestyle that values sustainability and respect for the earth. Whether hiking through nearby woods or enjoying a quiet morning on your porch, proximity to nature can reduce stress and enhance well-being.

Successfully transitioning to rural life involves more than just an appreciation for the outdoors; it requires building connections within your new community. Start by introducing yourself to neighbors and participating in local events. These interactions help you integrate and feel part of the community. Small towns often have a strong sense of camaraderie, and building relationships can provide a support network. Explore local resources and networks, such as farmers' markets, libraries, and community centers. These are great places to meet people and learn more about the area. Engaging with these resources can ease your transition and help you establish a fulfilling life in your new environment.

Reflection Activity: Embracing Change

Reflect on what excites you most and your apprehensions about the move. Write down ways you can address these concerns. Consider skills you might want to develop or hobbies you wish to pursue in your new setting. This activity can help clarify your goals and prepare you for the rewarding experiences that await in rural living.

The shift to rural or semi-rural living is a significant step, but it offers the chance to create a life that aligns more closely with your values and aspirations. Embrace the change, and you'll find a world rich with possibilities and personal growth.

1.4 CUSTOMIZATION POTENTIAL: DESIGNING YOUR DREAM SPACE

One of the most exciting aspects of building a barndominium is the sheer potential for customization. Imagine stepping into a home that reflects your soul, where every corner speaks to your tastes and lifestyle. Barndominiums offer a canvas for you to paint your dreams vividly, starting with unique interior layouts. The open spaces of these structures allow for creative configurations that break away from traditional home designs. Choose a sweeping open-concept layout that merges the kitchen, dining, and living areas into one harmonious space. This design encourages interaction and shared experiences, perfect for family gatherings or entertaining friends. Alternatively, consider incorporating distinctive features like sunken living rooms or raised platforms that create visual interest and define spaces without the need for walls.

Personalizing the exterior of your barndominium is equally rewarding. The choice of finishes can dramatically alter the appearance and feel of your home. Whether you lean toward a sleek, modern facade with metal cladding or prefer the warmth of wood paneling, the options are vast. Landscaping further enhances this personal touch, transforming your outdoor space into an extension of your home. Picture a wrap-around porch where you can enjoy morning coffee or a garden path leading to a secluded nook for quiet reflection. These elements balance practicality with aesthetics, ensuring that your home is as functional as it is beautiful.

Design flexibility is another hallmark of barndominiums. They invite innovative ideas that traditional homes might not accommodate. Consider utilizing lofts and mezzanines, which offer additional living space without expanding the building's footprint. These elevated areas can be cozy reading nooks, play areas, or compact home offices. The adaptability of barndominiums means you can tailor spaces to suit your needs, whether you're a growing family or a solo entrepreneur needing a creative studio. This flexibility ensures that your home evolves with you, adapting to changes in lifestyle and family dynamics without significant structural alterations.

Incorporating modern amenities into your barndominium bridges the gap between rustic charm and contemporary living. Smart home technologies provide convenience and efficiency, allowing you to control lighting, temperature, and security systems with a touch or voice command. These features enhance comfort and improve energy management, contributing to a sustainable living environment. Energy-efficient systems, such as advanced HVAC units or programmable thermostats, reduce energy consumption and lower utility bills. These modern conveniences seamlessly integrate into the rustic aesthetic of a barndominium, proving that high-tech and homespun can coexist beautifully.

Encouraging personalization in your barndominium goes beyond structural elements. It's about creating a space that resonates with who you are. Architectural styles vary widely, from industrial chic to farmhouse elegance, allowing you to infuse your personality into your home's design. Perhaps you favor a minimalist look with clean lines and neutral tones or a more eclectic approach with bold colors and diverse textures. The materials and finishes you choose are equally telling. Opt for natural stone for timeless durability or reclaimed wood for a rustic, environmentally conscious vibe. These choices reflect your values and lifestyle, making your home uniquely yours.

Ultimately, designing a barndominium allows you to express yourself and craft a living environment that serves your practical needs and inspires and delights you daily.

1.5 SUSTAINABILITY IN BARNDOMINIUMS: GREEN BUILDING TECHNIQUES

The appeal of a barndominium extends beyond its rustic charm and functional design. It offers an opportunity to live harmoniously with the environment through sustainable building practices. This approach not only reduces the ecological footprint but also enhances the efficiency and longevity of your home. Imagine constructing a living space that embodies the principles of sustainability, where every material and design choice contributes to a healthier planet. The use of recycled and sustainable materials is fundamental to this philosophy. By opting for reclaimed wood, recycled steel, or eco-friendly insulation, you conserve resources and add unique character to your home. These materials tell a story, connecting your living space to wider efforts to protect the environment.

Additionally, incorporating solar energy systems can significantly lower energy costs while reducing reliance on fossil fuels. Solar panels harness the sun's power, transforming it into clean, renewable energy to keep your home running efficiently. This shift towards renewable energy is a tangible step towards a more sustainable future.

Energy efficiency is another cornerstone of building a sustainable barndominium. The design should prioritize reducing energy consumption, which is both environmentally responsible and economically beneficial. Insulated wall panels and roofing are crucial in maintaining a consistent indoor temperature, minimizing the need for heating and cooling. By effectively sealing your home, you prevent energy loss, making it easier to maintain a comfortable environment year-round. Efficient heating and cooling systems further enhance this effort, using advanced technology to regulate temperature with minimal energy use. These systems are designed to adapt to your living habits, ensuring you only use energy when and where it's needed. The combination of these elements creates a home that is both comfortable and sustainable, reducing your carbon footprint while saving money on utility bills.

Water conservation is equally important in creating an eco-friendly barndominium. As water becomes an increasingly precious resource, using it wisely is imperative. Implementing rainwater harvesting systems can significantly reduce your dependency on municipal water supplies. These systems collect and store rainwater, which can be used for irrigation, flushing toilets, and washing clothes. By utilizing natural precipitation, you can reduce water usage and your environmental impact. Low-flow fixtures and appliances are another way to conserve water. These products are designed to deliver the same performance as standard models but use a fraction of the water. Incorporating them into your home ensures that every drop counts, minimizing waste and promoting sustainability.

Innovative technologies offer exciting possibilities for enhancing the sustainability of your barndominium. Smart grids and home automation systems are at the forefront of this technological revolution. These tools allow you to monitor and control energy usage in real-time, optimizing consumption to match your lifestyle and reducing waste. Imagine being able to adjust your home's energy settings from your smartphone, ensuring that you never use more power than necessary. This level of control increases efficiency and provides valuable insights into your energy habits, helping you make informed decisions about resource use. By integrating these technologies, you create a home that is not only modern but also deeply aligned with the principles of sustainable living.

Resource List: Essential Green Building Materials and Technologies

- Recycled and Sustainable Materials: Reclaimed wood, recycled steel, eco-friendly insulation
- Solar Energy Systems: Solar panels, energy storage solutions
- Energy Efficiency Techniques: Insulated wall panels, efficient heating and cooling systems
- Water Conservation Tools: Rainwater harvesting systems, low-flow fixtures, and appliances
- Innovative Technologies: Smart grids, home automation systems

This focus on sustainability transforms a barndominium into more than just a home; it becomes a statement of commitment to the environment. By embracing these green building techniques, you contribute to a future where living sustainably is the norm, not the exception.

1.6 COMMON MYTHS DEBUNKED: CLARIFYING MISCONCEPTIONS

In the world of barndominiums, myths abound, often rooted in misunderstanding or outdated perceptions. One of the most prevalent concerns is about their durability. Skeptics question whether these structures can withstand the test of time and the elements. However, the robust metal framing used in most barndominiums is a testament to their longevity. Steel frames offer unparalleled strength and resilience, far exceeding that of traditional wood framing. This material choice adds to the structural integrity and enhances safety and durability. Over time, the materials used in barndominiums have been refined and tested, proving that these homes are built to last. Many barndominium owners have reported minimal maintenance issues even after decades, a clear indicator of their enduring quality and reliability.

Another common misconception revolves around the costs associated with building and maintaining a barndominium. Some potential homeowners believe that the initial investment is prohibitive or that hidden expenses will arise at every turn. On the contrary, constructing a barndominium can be more budget-friendly than building a traditional home. The simplified design reduces construction costs significantly, allowing for more efficient use of resources and budget. While it's true that unforeseen costs can occur, a well-planned project can mitigate these risks. Understanding potential hidden expenses, such as land preparation or utility connections, allows for better financial planning. Barndominiums offer a clear cost advantage, making them a viable option for those seeking a high-quality home without the financial burden of conventional building methods.

Aesthetic concerns also arise when discussing barndominiums. Critics sometimes view them as purely functional, lacking in visual appeal. This couldn't be further from the truth. The design flexibility inherent in barndominiums allows for a wide range of modern and appealing styles. Whether you prefer sleek, minimalist designs or a rustic farmhouse look, there's a barndominium style to match your tastes. Customization options abound, from interior finishes to exterior facades, enabling homeowners to craft a beautiful and functional space. These homes can be tailored to fit any aesthetic, providing a unique combination of charm and modernity that rivals traditional houses. The ability to personalize every aspect ensures that a barndominium can be as visually stunning as it is practical.

Real-Life Success: A Case Study in Barndominium Living

Consider the case of a family who transformed an old barn into a vibrant living space, blending traditional elements with cutting-edge design. This project began as a simple idea: to create a home that respected the past while embracing the future. By using reclaimed wood and state-of-the-art technology, they crafted a space that is both warm and efficient. The family reports that their barndominium is comfortable and cost-effective, with energy bills significantly lower than in their previous residence. Their testimonial underscores the satisfaction and pride that come with creating a unique and enduring home. Visuals of their home showcase its stunning design, with expansive windows, elegant finishes, and a layout that encourages togetherness and creativity. This example illustrates that with careful planning and vision, a barndominium can transcend expectations, offering a living experience that is both beautiful and sustainable.

As misconceptions are dispelled, the true potential of barndominiums shines through. They offer a unique blend of durability, cost-effectiveness, and aesthetic appeal, making them an attractive option for modern homeowners. By understanding the realities and opportunities of barndominium living, you can confidently approach your project, knowing that you're investing in a home that offers more than just shelter. It's a lifestyle choice that reflects a commitment to innovation, sustainability, and personal expression. The myths may persist, but the truth is clear: barndominiums are a remarkable and viable housing option that continues to inspire and challenge conventional thinking.

CHAPTER TWO

PLANNING YOUR PROJECT
FROM VISION TO BLUEPRINT

Imagine standing on a piece of land where the horizon stretches endlessly and the air is filled with possibilities. This moment marks the beginning of your barndominium journey—a path toward crafting not just a home but a reflection of your dreams and aspirations. It's the chance to turn those dreams into blueprints and, eventually, walls that echo your lifestyle and values. As you stand there, the vision of your future home begins to crystalize. It's not just about building a structure; it's about creating a space that speaks to who you are and what you cherish.

2.1 CREATING THE VISION

Creating a vision for your barndominium starts with defining your objectives. Consider the long-term living needs that you and your family foresee. Are you planning for a space that accommodates a growing family or perhaps a peaceful retreat for two? Think about how life might change over the years and how your home can adapt to those changes. Visualizing these lifestyle enhancements is crucial. Maybe you dream of a spacious kitchen that becomes the heart of family gatherings or a cozy nook where you can unwind with a book. These visions guide the design and functionality of your future home, ensuring it meets current and future needs.

As you delve deeper into planning, it's essential to incorporate personal and family needs into your vision. Consider the unique requirements each member of your household might have. Do you need a home office for remote work or a dedicated workshop to nurture your hobbies? Perhaps you're planning for children or anticipating visits from extended family and friends. Accommodations for future family growth are vital, whether they involve extra bedrooms or versatile spaces that can evolve over time. Balancing these needs ensures your barndominium is not just a house but a home that supports everyone's lifestyle and aspirations.

Once you've established your needs, prioritize key features and amenities that will bring your vision to life. Open floor plans often top the list, offering flexibility and a sense of spaciousness that enhances everyday living. These layouts encourage interaction and adaptability, allowing you to define spaces according to your lifestyle. Sustainable systems and energy-efficient technologies are also essential considerations. Incorporating elements like solar panels or geothermal heating can reduce your ecological footprint and lower long-term costs. By focusing on these features, you create an environmentally responsible and economically sound home.

To help refine your ideas, consider creating a vision board. This tool is invaluable in transforming abstract concepts into tangible inspirations. Start by collecting images of design styles and layouts that resonate with you. Whether you're drawn to the industrial-chic aesthetic with exposed beams and metal accents or prefer the warmth of a modern farmhouse, these visuals serve as a foundation for your planning. Sketching initial floor plan concepts can further solidify your ideas, providing a blueprint for how various elements will come together. A vision board clarifies your goals and serves as a motivating reminder of the beautiful space you're working to create.

Reflection Activity: Vision Board Creation

Gather magazines, printouts, and any materials that inspire you. Spend time collecting images that capture the essence of your dream home. Arrange them on a board or digital platform, focusing on elements like color schemes, furniture styles, and architectural details. Use this vision board to guide your decisions and maintain focus on your ultimate goal.

As you embark on this planning phase, remember that the journey from vision to blueprint is as much about creativity as it is about practicality. Each decision you make brings you closer to a home that meets your needs and fulfills your dreams.

2.2 BUDGETING BASICS: ESTIMATING COSTS ACCURATELY

Building a barndominium is an exciting venture but requires careful financial planning to ensure success. Creating a comprehensive budget is a critical first step in this process. This means looking beyond the initial estimates and considering the full scope of expenses. Start by estimating the construction costs. These include land purchase, materials, labor, and any specialized services you may require. Consider the price of steel framing, roofing, and siding, as these are among the foundational elements of your barndominium. Labor costs will vary based on your location and the complexity of your design, so it's wise to obtain multiple quotes to get a realistic picture. Don't overlook the cost of permits and inspections necessary for compliance with local building codes. These fees can vary significantly, depending on your region and the specifics of your project. By accounting for them early, you avoid surprises that could disrupt your budget.

Hidden costs are another important consideration when budgeting for your barndominium. These unexpected expenses can quickly add up, straining your finances if not anticipated. Site preparation is a typical source of unforeseen costs. This includes grading the land to ensure proper drainage and clearing any debris or vegetation. Utility connections are another potential expense. Bringing electricity, water, and sewage services to a rural property can be more costly than in urban areas. Researching these costs and investing them into your budget early on is crucial. Weatherproofing and insulation are also significant expenses that are often underestimated. Proper insulation is vital for energy efficiency and comfort, especially in regions with extreme temperatures. Investing in high-quality weatherproofing materials will save money in the long run by reducing energy bills and maintenance needs.

Beyond these considerations, it's essential to remember that the interior finishes of your barndominium can also impact your budget significantly. From flooring to cabinetry, the choices you make will influence the overall cost. While it may be tempting to go for high-end finishes, consider the balance between quality and affordability. Plenty of options offer durability and style without breaking the bank. For those who are hands-on, tackling some of the interior work yourself can provide significant savings. However, be realistic about your skills and the time available to complete these tasks, as any mistakes could lead to additional expenses.

Budgeting Exercise: Crafting Your Financial Plan

Take time to list all the expected costs associated with building your barndominium. Break it down into categories such as materials, labor, permits, and interior finishes. Use this list to create a detailed financial plan, setting aside a contingency fund for unexpected expenses. This exercise helps you visualize the financial commitment and ensures you're prepared for all aspects of the project.

As you develop your budget, keep in mind that flexibility is key. Prices for materials can fluctuate due to market conditions, and unforeseen events can impact timelines. Building a buffer in your budget is wise to accommodate these variables. This approach not only prevents financial strain but also allows you to enjoy the process of creating your barndominium without the constant worry of overspending. Planning thoughtfully and thoroughly enables you to bring your vision to life while keeping your finances intact.

2.3 SELECTING YOUR SITE: FACTORS TO CONSIDER

Choosing the right location for your barndominium is a pivotal step that can shape your living experience for years to come. It's more than just finding a plot of land; it's about selecting a setting that complements your lifestyle and meets your practical needs. Start by considering proximity to work, schools, and essential amenities. If commuting is part of your daily routine, you'll want a site that offers easy access to major roads or public transportation.

Families with school-aged children should also factor in the distance to local schools and the quality of education available. For some, being close to grocery stores, healthcare facilities, and recreational areas is crucial for convenience and quality of life.

Climate plays a significant role in influencing your design choices and material selection. In regions with extreme temperatures, you might prioritize insulation and heating or cooling systems to ensure comfort year-round. Meanwhile, areas prone to heavy rainfall or snow might require specific roofing materials and drainage solutions to protect your investment. Assessing the climate not only aids in creating a comfortable living space but also helps in planning for long-term sustainability and energy efficiency.

The physical characteristics of the land itself are equally important. Begin by analyzing the soil quality and drainage capacity of the site. Good soil is foundational for stability, ensuring your barndominium stands strong over time. Poor drainage can lead to waterlogging and structural issues, so choosing a site that naturally manages water well or can be modified to do so is vital. The topography of the land also affects the feasibility of construction. Flat terrain simplifies the building process, but gently rolling hills can offer unique aesthetic advantages, providing stunning views or natural landscaping opportunities. Accessibility is another factor to consider. Ensure that vehicles, especially construction machinery, can easily reach the site during the building phase and consider future access for maintenance.

Understanding local zoning laws and legal restrictions is crucial. Zoning regulations dictate what can be built where, so it's imperative to ensure that your site complies with these laws. Some areas may have restrictions on building types or sizes, which can impact your plans. Before finalizing a purchase, verify that the land is zoned appropriately for a barndominium and that any necessary permits can be obtained. This step prevents costly legal challenges down the line and ensures your project proceeds smoothly.

Thinking long-term about your site choice can significantly enhance your living experience. Consider the potential for future expansion if your needs change over time. Whether you envision adding a guest house, a detached garage, or expanding your living space, choose a site that can accommodate such growth. Ample space for outdoor amenities like gardens, patios, or a pool adds value and enjoyment to your property. Planning for these possibilities from the outset ensures that your barndominium can adapt to your evolving lifestyle.

In summary, selecting the right site for your barndominium involves carefully balancing personal preferences, practical considerations, and long-term vision. By evaluating location preferences, assessing land characteristics, understanding zoning laws, and considering future expansion potential, you lay the groundwork for a successful and satisfying barndominium project.

2.4 DESIGNING FOR MULTI-FUNCTIONALITY: SPACE PLANNING TIPS

When envisioning your barndominium, think of it as a dynamic space that can adapt to your evolving needs. The essence of multi-functionality lies in crafting rooms that can transform effortlessly. Consider a guest room that doubles as a home office. By day, it is a productive workspace with a desk and the necessary tech setup. It transforms into a cozy sleeping area with a comfortable pull-out bed at night. This flexibility is invaluable, especially when space is at a premium or you anticipate frequent visitors.

Open areas that cater to changing needs are a hallmark of smart design. Imagine a large living space that serves as a family room, dining area, and play zone, all within the same open-concept layout. This allows for continuous transitions between activities, whether you're hosting a dinner party or enjoying a quiet movie night. Such spaces encourage interaction and can be easily reconfigured to accommodate different events. The key is to maintain a balance between openness and functionality, ensuring that each zone is clearly defined yet flexible enough to serve multiple purposes.

Incorporating flexible design elements is crucial to achieving versatility. Sliding partitions or movable walls offer an innovative way to alter the layout of a room without permanent construction. These features allow you to create privacy when needed or open up spaces for larger gatherings. Modular furniture systems, too, are game-changers. Think of sectionals that can be rearranged to suit the occasion or tables that adjust in height for various uses. These pieces provide both form and function, allowing your barndominium to adapt to your lifestyle seamlessly.

Maximizing efficiency in space usage involves thoughtful planning of storage and layout. Creative storage solutions, like built-in shelves and under-stair storage, help keep clutter at bay while making the most of available space. Consider multi-level layouts if your barndominium design includes high ceilings. A loft can serve as a reading nook or additional sleeping area, using vertical space without encroaching on the main living areas. These strategies enhance your home's functionality and aesthetic appeal, ensuring that every inch is utilized effectively.

Balancing privacy and openness requires a nuanced approach. Zoned areas for different functions are essential for maintaining order and flow. Rugs, lighting, or furniture placement can delineate spaces without the need for walls. Noise-reducing materials, such as acoustic panels or heavy drapes, can help manage sound in open areas and ensure privacy when needed. These design techniques create a harmonious environment where communal and private spaces coexist beautifully, catering to both social gatherings and quiet moments.

2.5 BALANCING AESTHETICS AND FUNCTIONALITY: DESIGN HARMONY

Creating a barndominium that flawlessly blends aesthetics with functionality requires a thoughtful approach to design. Achieving a cohesive look means harmonizing color schemes and materials to ensure everything complements each other. Imagine walking into a space where the palette of warm grays and deep blues gracefully transitions from the living room to the kitchen. Each room flows into the next, creating a sense of unity and continuity. Using materials like reclaimed wood and stone adds texture and warmth and ties the entire space together, offering a timeless appeal that resonates with both rustic and modern sensibilities. Every piece of furniture, every fixture, plays a part in this symphony of design, ensuring that your home is visually appealing and feels complete and intentional.

Personal expression is vital to any home, and your barndominium should reflect your unique tastes and preferences. Selecting themes that resonate personally allows you to infuse your space with elements that speak to who you are. Whether you gravitate towards a minimalist aesthetic or a more eclectic mix, the key is to customize fixtures and finishes to echo your style. This might mean choosing a particular type of lighting fixture that adds character or selecting cabinetry that reflects your love for craftsmanship. These choices become the fingerprints of your personality across your home. They transform a basic structure into a personal sanctuary, a place where every detail has significance and meaning.

Practicality is as important as beauty in any design, and focusing on usability ensures your barndominium functions as it should. Ergonomic kitchen and bathroom setups are crucial, making daily tasks easier and more enjoyable. Consider how you move through these spaces and how they can be optimized for efficiency and comfort. Easy access to utilities and amenities means placing things where they make sense, reducing unnecessary steps, and keeping everything within reach. A well-designed layout considers the flow of daily life, ensuring that each room serves its purpose effectively without sacrificing style or comfort.

Integrating natural elements into your design creates a harmonious living environment that connects the indoors with the outdoors. Large windows are a wonderful way to bring in natural light, illuminating your space and making it feel open and inviting. They also provide views of the surrounding landscape, allowing you to enjoy nature's beauty from the comfort of your home. Seamless transitions to outdoor living areas, such as through glass doors that open onto a patio or garden, extend your living space beyond the walls of your home. These transitions encourage a lifestyle that embraces the beauty of the natural world, offering a sense of peace and tranquility. They also provide outdoor entertaining and relaxation opportunities, enhancing your overall living experience.

2.6 UNDERSTANDING ZONING LAWS AND RESTRICTIONS

Navigating the labyrinth of zoning laws and building restrictions can seem daunting, but it's a crucial step in bringing your barndominium dreams to life. Each region has its own set of rules that dictate what can be built, where, and how. These regulations are designed to ensure safety, community standards, and environmental protection. Start by researching local regulations to identify the zoning classifications relevant to barndominiums in your area. Understanding these classifications will help you determine whether your intended site is suitable for residential use or if it falls under agricultural or commercial classifications that might restrict building. Familiarize yourself with the building codes that apply to your project. These codes encompass everything from structural integrity to energy efficiency standards. They ensure your barndominium will be safe, functional, and compliant with local laws.

Securing the necessary permits is the next step in the process. Applying for building permits involves gathering a range of documentation, including site plans, architectural drawings, and proof of compliance with zoning laws. It's important to check with your local planning department to understand exactly what is required. Some regions may require additional approvals for elements like septic systems or electrical work. Once you have all the required documentation, submit your application to the appropriate local authority. This step can take time, so it's wise to factor in potential waiting periods when planning your construction timeline. Be prepared to address any questions or requests for additional information from the permitting office, as this can speed up the approval process.

Legal challenges are not uncommon in the world of construction, and being prepared for them is key. Sometimes, your design may not fully comply with existing regulations. In such cases, you might need to apply for a variance, which is a request for an exception to the zoning rules. This process involves demonstrating that your project will not adversely affect the surrounding area and that there are unique circumstances justifying the deviation. Negotiating with local planning authorities requires patience and a willingness to compromise. Engaging in open communication and presenting well-reasoned arguments can often lead to favorable outcomes, allowing your project to move forward without unnecessary delays.

Staying updated on changes in zoning laws and building codes is essential for both the construction phase and the future maintenance of your barndominium. Zoning laws can change over time, and it's important to be aware of any updates that might affect your property. Joining local community planning meetings can provide valuable insights into proposed changes and offer a platform for voicing any concerns you might have. Subscribing to updates from local zoning boards ensures you receive timely information about any revisions to regulations or building codes. This proactive approach helps you avoid legal complications and ensures that your barndominium remains compliant with all local requirements.

As we wrap up this chapter, remember that understanding zoning laws is as important as any other part of your planning process. With a clear grasp of the rules and the right permits in hand, you're well on your way to creating a legally sound and beautifully crafted home.

CHAPTER THREE

NAVIGATING PERMITS AND REGULATIONS

Picture this: you're standing at the edge of a plot of land, envisioning the barndominium that will soon rise from the ground. The air is filled with the promise of new beginnings. Yet, before that first nail is hammered, there's an invisible gate to pass through—building codes and permits. These aren't just bureaucratic hurdles; they are the guardians of safety and quality, ensuring that your dream home doesn't become a nightmare. Understanding these codes can seem daunting, but they're designed to protect you, your investment, and your future home. They ensure that your barndominium is not only beautiful but also safe and sound, ready to stand the test of time and nature.

3.1 PERMITTING AND REGULATION: WHY IS THIS PART SO IMPORTANT?

Building codes serve a crucial purpose in the construction world. They are the backbone of a project's safety and structural integrity. At their core, building codes are detailed regulations that specify the minimum standards for construction. These standards cover a wide range of aspects, from the strength of the materials used to the design of the building itself. Adhering to these codes ensures your barndominium is built to withstand natural forces such as wind and earthquakes, providing a safe shelter for you and your loved ones. Beyond structural integrity, these codes also protect public health and welfare. They dictate the installation of essential systems like plumbing and electrical wiring, ensuring they are both efficient and safe. Imagine the chaos of a home without these standards—a place where electrical systems fail or plumbing backs up. Building codes prevent such scenarios, creating a living environment that is both functional and secure.

To navigate the maze of building codes effectively, it's important to identify the key elements you need to know. Structural requirements are at the forefront, dictating how a building must be constructed to ensure its stability. This includes specifications for load-bearing walls, the foundation's design, and the roof's strength. Fire safety is another critical component. Codes require buildings to have features such as smoke detectors, fire extinguishers, and proper emergency exits. These regulations are particularly vital in structures like barndominiums, which may combine living and working spaces. Ensuring fire safety means you're protecting your property and safeguarding lives. Emergency access is also mandated, requiring clear pathways and exits that allow for quick evacuation if needed. These elements work together to create a safe and resilient environment that can handle emergencies without compromising safety.

Understanding the distinction between national and local codes is essential. National standards provide a baseline of safety and quality across the country. They are developed by professional societies and updated regularly to incorporate new best practices. However, each state, city, or county has the authority to adapt these standards to address local needs and conditions. This is why local codes can vary significantly. For instance, a barndominium built in a coastal area might need to meet stricter requirements for wind resistance compared to one in an inland region. Consulting local building departments is crucial to ensure compliance with these adaptations. They provide guidance on specific requirements and help you understand how national standards are applied locally. This knowledge is key to avoiding costly mistakes and ensuring your project proceeds smoothly.

Beginners often misinterpret building codes, which can lead to problems down the line. One common misunderstanding is misjudging the scope of the requirements. Some may assume that only large projects must comply with codes, overlooking that even small modifications can be subject to these regulations. Overlooking updates or amendments to codes is another pitfall. Building codes are not static; they evolve to incorporate new technologies and safety measures. Failing to stay informed about these changes can result in non-compliance, which might necessitate costly modifications or even fines. It's vital to approach building codes with a comprehensive understanding and a proactive mindset, ensuring that your barndominium meets today's standards and is prepared for future updates. Keep in mind that in many areas, building inspections are required to ensure that the codes are being followed correctly.

In addition, some rural areas may have few or no building requirements. In this instance, it is up to you to ensure your work or the work of your contractors, is at the same level of safety and quality required at a city level. This will save headaches down the road to ensure quality work or even pass a home inspection if you sell the barndominium at a later date.

3.2 SECURING NECESSARY PERMITS: STEP-BY-STEP GUIDE

Stepping into the world of permits might feel like navigating a complex maze, but with a clear plan, it becomes manageable. To start, gather all the required documents and plans. This includes detailed site plans, architectural drawings, and any environmental assessments if needed. These documents form the backbone of your application, showcasing your vision and how it aligns with local regulations. Having these documents ready demonstrates preparedness and streamlines the process, reducing potential delays. Ensure each document is accurate and complete, as omissions or mistakes can lead to setbacks. Once your paperwork is in order, submit your application to the relevant authorities. This might be your city's building department or, in rural areas, the county office. Each jurisdiction will have its own procedures, so it's crucial to follow their specific guidelines closely.

Understanding timelines and waiting periods is crucial to managing expectations. On average, processing times for building permits can range from a few weeks to several months. Factors such as your project's complexity, the permitting office's current workload, and specific local requirements can all impact this timeline. It's not uncommon for delays to occur, especially in areas experiencing a construction boom. Therefore, patience and flexibility are essential. Consider building a buffer into your project timeline to accommodate these potential delays. This approach prevents frustration and allows you to plan other aspects of your build more effectively, ensuring everything aligns once approval is granted.

Inspections are a key part of the permitting process, acting as checkpoints to ensure compliance at various stages of construction. Before you even break ground, a pre-construction site inspection may be required. This initial assessment ensures that your site is ready for development and that all preparatory work aligns with your plans. As construction progresses, additional inspections will be necessary. These typically include checks of the foundation, framing, electrical, and plumbing systems. Each inspection serves to verify that the work meets code requirements and is structurally sound. The final inspection occurs once construction is complete, ensuring everything is in place before you occupy your barndominium. These inspections are not just formalities but assurances that your home is safe and built to last.

Consider a few strategic steps to increase your chances of a successful application. Double-checking your application forms for errors is a simple but effective way to avoid unnecessary delays. Mistakes can slow down the process, leading to back-and-forth communication with the permitting office. Pre-consultation meetings with building officials can also be incredibly beneficial. These meetings allow for clarification of any uncertainties and receiving feedback on your plans before submission. Building a rapport with these officials can lead to smoother interactions throughout the permitting process. They can offer insights that might not be immediately obvious, helping you refine your approach and align your project with local expectations. Engaging in this proactive communication can make the permitting process less daunting and more collaborative.

3.3 OVERCOMING BUREAUCRATIC HURDLES: TIPS AND TRICKS

Navigating the permit process can feel like wading through a bureaucratic swamp. Lengthy approval processes are one of the most common hurdles you'll face. It's not unusual for an application to sit on someone's desk longer than expected, especially in busy municipalities. This can be frustrating, but understanding that these delays are often due to high volumes of applications can help manage expectations. Inconsistent communication from authorities adds another layer of complexity. You might find yourself receiving different information from different departments, leading to confusion. This lack of coordination can make it difficult to determine exactly what's needed or when to expect a response.

To mitigate these delays, regular follow-ups with permit offices are crucial. A simple phone call or email can keep your application moving forward and show you're engaged with the process. Persistence is key; don't hesitate to be politely persistent in seeking updates. Building a buffer into your project timeline is another smart strategy. You can plan around potential delays withoutderailing your entire schedule by anticipating potential delays. This buffer provides breathing room, allowing you to adjust without stress when things don't go exactly as planned. While it may extend your timeline initially, it can prevent more significant disruptions down the line.

Building inspectors play a significant role in the permit process. They are the ones who will ensure that your project meets all required standards at various stages. Scheduling inspections at key milestones is crucial. Inspections are typically required before you move from one phase to the next, such as before drywall goes up or before final occupancy. Addressing inspector feedback promptly is also vital. If they find issues, resolving them quickly can prevent further delays. Inspectors aren't just gatekeepers but allies in ensuring your barndominium is safe and compliant. Understanding their role and working with them can make a significant difference in the smooth progression of your project.

Proactive communication is your best tool against bureaucratic hurdles. Maintaining open lines of communication with officials can help clarify expectations and keep everyone on the same page. Documenting all interactions and agreements clearly records what's been discussed and agreed upon. This can be invaluable if discrepancies arise later. Utilizing digital tools for efficient communication, such as email or project management software, can streamline these interactions, ensuring that nothing falls through the cracks. These tools facilitate communication and help organize documentation, making it easier to reference past conversations and agreements when needed.

3.4 AVOIDING LEGAL PITFALLS: STAYING COMPLIANT

Building a barndominium is thrilling, but remaining vigilant against legal pitfalls derailing your progress is crucial. One of the most common issues is proceeding without the proper permits. This oversight can lead to significant headaches down the road, including stop-work orders and hefty fines. Permits are not merely bureaucratic hurdles—they are legal requirements that ensure your project adheres to safety and zoning standards. Without them, your entire build could be jeopardized. Another frequent compliance issue arises when modifications are made to approved plans without consulting the appropriate authorities. Even minor changes can require approval, and ignoring this step can lead to complications, including necessary rework or legal action.

Maintaining compliance requires diligence and foresight. Regularly reviewing your project plans against the approved documents is a straightforward yet effective strategy. This practice ensures that any deviations are caught early and addressed before they become significant issues. Engaging professionals, such as architects or contractors, is advisable for complex legal matters. These experts can provide guidance and ensure that all aspects of your build meet local requirements. Their experience and knowledge are invaluable in navigating the intricacies of construction law, which can often be overwhelming for beginners.

The consequences of non-compliance can be severe and far-reaching. Fines and penalties are immediate and tangible repercussions, but the long-term effects can be even more damaging. Non-compliance can lead to legal actions that halt construction, resulting in delays and additional costs. In extreme cases, you might be forced to undo completed work to align your project with legal standards. Such setbacks are frustrating and can strain your budget and timeline. The peace of mind that comes from knowing your project is compliant far outweighs the risks of cutting corners.

A robust documentation process is your best defense against potential legal issues. Archiving all permits and inspection reports is crucial. These documents serve as proof of compliance and can protect you in case of disputes. Keeping a log of communications and decisions made throughout the project helps maintain clarity and accountability. This record can be invaluable if questions arise about why certain choices were made. It's a simple yet powerful way to ensure that every step of your build is transparent and traceable. Adequate documentation safeguards your project against legal challenges and contributes to a smoother construction process overall.

3.5 UNDERSTANDING REGIONAL VARIATIONS: LOCAL REGULATIONS

As you embark on your barndominium project, it's vital to understand that where you build can significantly influence how you build. Regulations vary widely from one region to another, often shaped by local climate conditions and environmental priorities. In coastal areas, for instance, building materials must often withstand high humidity and the corrosive effects of salt air. These conditions necessitate using weather-resistant materials that might not be required inland. Conversely, in colder inland regions, insulation becomes a priority to combat frigid temperatures, influencing the types of materials and construction techniques you'll consider. Climate is not the only factor; however, local environmental laws play a crucial role. In some areas, for instance, regulations protect historical sites or natural habitats, imposing restrictions that can dictate everything from the size and placement of structures to the types of materials used.

Consider the stark differences between coastal and inland building requirements. Coastal regions, often prone to hurricanes or severe storms, might require structures to have fortified roofing and additional anchoring systems. These measures ensure resilience against high winds and flooding. Inland, where such weather events are rare, the regulatory focus might shift towards energy efficiency and insulation, addressing the challenges of maintaining comfortable indoor temperatures in extreme cold or heat. Similarly, urban and rural areas can have vastly different zoning laws. Urban settings might impose strict guidelines on building heights and designs to maintain aesthetic consistency and manage population density. In contrast, rural areas might offer more freedom, though they can also come with their own set of regulations focused on preserving open spaces and agricultural land.

Researching local regulations is essential to understanding these variations and ensuring compliance with local laws. One effective method is utilizing online municipal resources. Many local governments provide detailed zoning maps, building codes, and permit requirements on their websites. These resources can give you a comprehensive overview of what's expected in your area. Additionally, consulting local planning offices or professionals can provide invaluable insights. These experts can clarify complex regulations and guide you through the nuances of local building requirements. They're often familiar with the common pitfalls and can help you avoid costly mistakes that could delay your project.

Regional codes can heavily influence your design choices. For example, the roofing materials you select might need to accommodate heavy snowfall or intense sun exposure, depending on your location. In regions with significant snowfall, roofs may require a steep pitch to prevent snow accumulation, whereas in sunny climates, reflective materials might be recommended to reduce heat absorption. Local codes can also dictate exterior aesthetics, particularly in historic districts or environmentally sensitive areas. You might find restrictions on color schemes or using specific materials to preserve the area's character or ecological balance. These regulations ensure that new constructions harmonize with their surroundings, contributing to the community's overall aesthetic and environmental goals.

3.6 REAL-LIFE CASE STUDIES: NAVIGATING PERMITS SUCCESSFULLY

Imagine the situation of a couple in the Midwest, determined to build their barndominium on a plot of family land. They faced a labyrinth of local regulations and were initially overwhelmed by the complexity of the permitting process. Yet, their perseverance through intricate bureaucratic scenarios showcased the power of diligent preparation and adaptability. They navigated unexpected regulatory changes by meticulously organizing their documents and seeking expert advice. One such change was a mid-project amendment in local environmental codes that required additional assessments. Instead of succumbing to frustration, they adapted by consulting an environmental engineer who helped revise their plans to meet the new requirements. Their success rested on thorough preparation and strategic flexibility, demonstrating that the right approach can overcome even the most daunting challenges.

Another inspiring story comes from a single parent in the Pacific Northwest who tackled the unique challenge of building amidst stringent zoning laws. Her project faced hurdles when local authorities revised regulations to protect a nearby wetland. This change threatened to halt her dream home's construction. However, she crafted a solution by showcasing creativity and a proactive attitude. She redesigned her site plan to incorporate natural landscaping that complied with new regulations and enhanced the local ecosystem. Her experience highlights the importance of creative solutions in the face of regulatory challenges and underscores the value of understanding the broader environmental context of a building site.

Key takeaways from these cases emphasize the significance of thorough preparation and the willingness to adapt plans when necessary. Detailed research and planning were crucial; both parties invested time in understanding the landscape of local regulations before breaking ground. They leveraged professional advice when needed, recognizing that experts like structural engineers or environmental consultants could provide invaluable insights. These professionals helped interpret complex codes and offered solutions aligned with personal and regulatory goals. By engaging with these experts early in the process, they avoided potential pitfalls that could have derailed their projects.

Challenges such as navigating unexpected regulatory changes and balancing project goals with constraints were prevalent in each case. The lessons learned underscore the importance of building strong relationships with local officials. These relationships facilitated open communication, which was vital when surprises arose. Understanding the perspective of local authorities allowed these individuals to align their projects with community objectives, easing the path to approval. By maintaining this rapport, they anticipated potential hurdles and addressed them proactively, ensuring smoother progress.

For readers embarking on their barndominium projects, these real-world experiences offer several actionable insights. Building a rapport with local officials can lead to more collaborative interactions and provide clarity when navigating complex codes. Additionally, utilizing case study insights to anticipate potential hurdles can prepare you for unforeseen challenges. Consider regularly reviewing local regulations and being open to adjusting plans if necessary. This flexibility can be the difference between a stalled project and a successful build. These strategies enhance the likelihood of a successful permit process and contribute to a rewarding and fulfilling building experience.

As we wrap up our exploration of navigating permits and regulations, it's clear that while the path may be fraught with challenges, the rewards of perseverance, creativity, and collaboration are immense. Each step forward strengthens your foundation, paving the way for a successful barndominium project. With the groundwork laid, the next chapter will guide you through the construction phase, turning those approved plans into your dream home.

CHAPTER FOUR

BUILDING YOUR TEAM
CONTRACTORS AND DIY APPROACHES

I magine standing amidst the skeletal frame of your future barndominium, the morning sun casting long shadows over the work site. The anticipation is palpable, yet the task ahead is monumental. Building a barndominium requires more than just vision and enthusiasm—it demands a reliable team of contractors. These individuals will be your partners, turning your dreams into tangible reality. Finding the right contractors is crucial, as they bring expertise and experience to navigate the complexities of construction. Begin by establishing robust selection criteria to evaluate potential candidates effectively.

4.1 HIRING CONTRACTORS: WHAT YOU SHOULD LOOK FOR

When evaluating contractors, licensing and insurance are non-negotiable. These credentials protect you and your project, ensuring the contractor is legally authorized and financially covered to perform the work. Licensing indicates a level of professionalism and adherence to industry standards, while insurance provides a safety net against potential mishaps. Next, assess their experience with barndominium projects specifically. This niche construction type requires a unique set of skills and knowledge. Contractors with a history of successful barndominium build will be more adept at handling the particular challenges these projects present, from managing open-concept designs to integrating sustainable materials and technologies.

Conducting thorough background checks is essential. Start by requesting references and reviews from past clients. Speaking with previous customers gives you firsthand insights into the contractor's reliability, work quality, and professionalism. Ask about their punctuality, adherence to budget, and problem-solving abilities during unforeseen issues. Additionally, investigate any legal disputes or complaints filed against them. This research can reveal potential red flags and help you avoid contractors with a litigation history or unsatisfactory work. A contractor's reputation is built on their past performance, and a diligent background check ensures you align with someone whose track record inspires confidence.

The interview process is an opportunity to gauge the contractor's compatibility with your project. Ask about their availability and project timelines to ensure they can meet your schedule. Discuss their approach to problem-solving, as construction inevitably involves unexpected challenges. How they handle such situations reveals their adaptability and resourcefulness. Effective communication during this stage sets the tone for your working relationship, highlighting whether they listen to your needs and articulate their processes clearly. A contractor who values transparent communication and demonstrates a proactive attitude will likely be a valuable partner throughout the construction.

Negotiating terms and pricing is a critical step in formalizing the contractor relationship. Begin by comparing quotes from multiple contractors. This comparison helps you find competitive rates and highlights variations in proposed services and timelines. Understand the payment schedules and terms fully. Some contractors require a deposit upfront, while others might have milestone-based payments. Clarifying these terms prevents misunderstandings and ensures financial transparency. Remember, the cheapest bid is not always the best choice; weigh the cost against the contractor's experience, reputation, and your comfort level with their working style.

Reflection Section: Crafting Your Contractor Evaluation Checklist

Create a checklist to streamline your contractor evaluation process. Include items like verifying licensing and insurance, assessing barndominium experience, conducting background checks, and preparing interview questions. Use this checklist to maintain consistency and objectivity as you evaluate each potential contractor, ensuring you make an informed and confident decision.

4.2 THE DIY APPROACH: WHAT YOU CAN DO YOURSELF

Taking on parts of your barndominium project yourself can be rewarding and cost-effective. It's a chance to infuse personal touches into your home while saving on labor costs. Start with tasks that are manageable and within your skill set. Simple interior painting and decorating are excellent DIY options. With the right tools and patience, you can transform a space with color, adding personality without needing professional help. Similarly, landscaping and gardening offer opportunities to shape your outdoor space, creating an environment that complements the rustic charm of your barndominium. These tasks enhance the aesthetic appeal and provide a sense of ownership and pride in your home.

Before diving into DIY projects, take a moment to assess your skills and limitations. This honest evaluation is crucial to avoid taking on more than you can handle. Reflect on past experiences with similar projects. Have you painted a room before? Maybe you've dabbled in gardening or installed a few shelves. These experiences can guide you in deciding which tasks are feasible. Recognizing when to seek professional help is equally important. Some projects, like electrical work or complex plumbing, require specialized skills and can pose safety risks if done incorrectly. Knowing your limits ensures you maintain quality and safety, preventing costly mistakes and ensuring a smooth building process.

Gather the necessary tools and resources once you've identified the DIY tasks you're comfortable with. Having the right equipment makes all the difference. Invest in quality brushes, rollers, and drop cloths to achieve a professional finish for painting. Landscaping might require tools like shovels, pruners, and a wheelbarrow. Consider renting more expensive items, such as power tools, to save money while still accessing what you need. Online tutorials and guides can be invaluable resources, providing step-by-step instructions and tips from experienced DIYers. Websites, video platforms, and forums are excellent places to find support and inspiration, helping you build confidence in your abilities.

Time management is key to balancing DIY efforts with other responsibilities. Creating a realistic project timeline helps keep you on track. Break down tasks into manageable sections and allocate specific days or weekends to work on them. This structured approach prevents overwhelm and allows you to focus on one task at a time. Allocate time for learning and practice, especially if you're tackling something new. Practicing techniques on a smaller scale before applying them to your barndominium can enhance your skills and ensure better results. Remember to invest time in trial and error, as learning often involves making and correcting mistakes. This preparation leads to a more enjoyable and successful DIY experience.

4.3 CONTRACTOR CONTRACTS: KEY ELEMENTS TO INCLUDE

Creating a solid contract with your chosen contractor is critical in construction. It serves as the blueprint for your working relationship, detailing the expectations and responsibilities of both parties. Begin by clearly defining the scope of work and establishing a realistic project timeline. This section should outline every task the contractor is responsible for, from laying the foundation to the final coat of paint. Being specific about deadlines helps prevent misunderstandings and sets a clear path for project progression. Including penalties for missed deadlines can provide additional motivation for timely completion. It's essential that both parties agree on these terms before work begins to ensure harmony and clarity.

Payment terms and conditions are another vital component of your contract. Clarity in this section prevents future disputes and ensures financial transactions proceed smoothly. Specify the project's total cost, breaking it down into stages if necessary. This might include initial deposits, progress payments, and the final payment upon project completion. Be transparent about the payment schedule, detailing when each installment is due and the acceptable methods of payment. Consider including a clause for withholding payment if work does not meet agreed-upon standards, providing a measure of protection for your investment. Clear financial arrangements foster trust and accountability, paving the way for a successful partnership.

Materials and specifications need clear documentation in your contract. This section should list the specific brands and quality standards of all materials to be used. Whether it's the type of wood for your floors or the brand of paint for your walls, precision here ensures you receive exactly what you expect. Discuss who will be responsible for purchasing these materials and who will cover the costs. It's often beneficial for the contractor to handle procurement, as they typically have access to better prices and know the most reliable suppliers. However, if you prefer to source materials yourself, specify this in the contract. This clarity prevents disputes over costs and quality, ensuring that both parties are aligned in their vision for the project.

Defining responsibilities and expectations is key to a smooth project flow. Your contract should outline the contractor's responsibilities for site management, including securing permits, managing subcontractors, and ensuring site safety. It should also clarify your responsibilities as the homeowner, such as providing access to the site and making timely decisions regarding design changes. Both parties should understand their roles to minimize friction and maintain a productive working environment. Open communication about these responsibilities helps build a collaborative relationship where each party respects and fulfills their commitments.

Addressing conflict resolution procedures in the contract is prudent. Construction projects can be unpredictable, and having a plan for handling disputes or changes can save time and frustration. Consider including clauses for mediation or arbitration, providing a structured way to resolve disagreements without litigation. This approach can be less adversarial and more cost-effective. Additionally, establish procedures for change orders or project modifications. These should outline how changes are proposed, approved, and funded, ensuring that any alterations to the original plan are managed smoothly. These processes provide peace of mind and keep the project on track, even when challenges arise.

4.4 MANAGING YOUR TEAM: EFFECTIVE COMMUNICATION

In the midst of a barndominium project, communication stands as the backbone of your success. Establishing clear communication channels with your team is paramount. It's about creating a seamless flow of information, ensuring that everyone remains aligned and informed throughout the process. Scheduling regular progress meetings is one way to achieve this. These meetings provide a forum for updates, discussions, and the resolution of any issues that may have arisen. They ensure that all team members are on the same page, fostering a sense of unity and purpose. It's an opportunity to reinforce objectives, celebrate milestones, and address any concerns that might slow progress. Beyond face-to-face meetings, utilizing digital communication tools can keep everyone connected. Platforms allowing instant messaging, file sharing, and real-time updates are invaluable. They help bridge the gap between meetings, keeping the momentum going and allowing for quick resolutions to any emerging issues.

Setting expectations and priorities from the outset is another crucial element of effective communication. This involves clearly articulating your project goals and priorities to your team. Providing a detailed project brief is a good start. This document should outline the vision for the project, the specific outcomes desired, and the overarching timeline. It acts as a roadmap, guiding everyone involved towards the same destination. Within this brief, key milestones and deadlines should be highlighted, serving as checkpoints that help keep the project on track. By clearly communicating these priorities, you ensure all team members understand what is expected of them and can align their efforts accordingly.

Fostering a collaborative environment is essential for maintaining a positive and productive team dynamic. Building rapport and trust with your contractors and team members is foundational. When people feel valued and respected, they are more likely to contribute positively and go the extra mile. Encouraging feedback and suggestions from all parties involved can lead to innovative solutions and a stronger sense of ownership. Creating an atmosphere where team members feel comfortable sharing their thoughts and ideas is essential. This collaboration not only enhances the quality of the work but also builds a sense of camaraderie and mutual respect among the team.

Monitoring and adjusting communication strategies as the project progresses is essential to maintaining effectiveness. Regularly evaluate how well your communication methods are working and be open to making adjustments as needed. Address any misunderstandings promptly to prevent them from escalating into larger issues. This might involve clarifying instructions, revisiting project goals, or simply checking in with team members to ensure everyone is on the same page. Adapting communication styles to suit different team members can also enhance understanding and cooperation. Some individuals respond better to detailed emails, while others prefer quick, verbal updates. Flexibility in your approach helps accommodate your team's diverse needs and preferences, fostering a more harmonious working environment.

Effective communication is the oil that keeps the gears turning smoothly in the heart of a barndominium build. It ensures that all efforts are aligned, that challenges are met with collective wisdom, and that each milestone brings the team closer to realizing the vision.

4.5 ENSURING QUALITY WORKMANSHIP: MONITORING PROGRESS

As your barndominium begins to take shape, ensuring quality workmanship becomes paramount. Establishing clear quality benchmarks from the outset is crucial. Define what acceptable tolerances and finish levels look like for your project. Consider every detail, from the smoothness of drywall to the precision of tile work. These benchmarks are your standard, a measure against which all work is assessed. Regular inspections of completed work against these standards help maintain consistency and quality. For the best results, plan to be onsite for your construction project once a day. It is much easier to fix a wall in the wrong place, a missing window or door if it is caught immediately. If work progresses too far past a mistake, there can be significant issue in making corrections. You'll want to ensure that every element of construction meets or exceeds your expectations, ultimately leading to a satisfying final product.

Frequent site visits are not just beneficial; they're necessary. They allow you to observe work practices and ensure adherence to established safety protocols. On these visits, check the progress against your project timeline. Is the framing complete? Have the plumbing and electrical systems been installed as planned? Regular visits provide you with firsthand knowledge of what's happening on-site, allowing you to catch potential issues early. It's also an opportunity to engage with your team, fostering a positive working environment while staying informed about the project's status. Your presence signals commitment and keeps everyone aligned with your vision.

Documenting work progress and any issues that arise is a practical step in maintaining control over your project. Take photos and detailed notes during each site visit. These records serve as a valuable reference, illustrating the project's evolution and highlighting areas needing attention. Maintain a log of any issues or delays encountered, noting how they were addressed. This log not only aids in tracking progress but also provides a clear account of the project's history. Should disputes or questions arise later, this documentation offers clarity and supports effective communication with your contractors.

When quality issues do surface, addressing them promptly is vital. Open communication with your contractors is key. Discuss any concerns directly and constructively, focusing on solutions rather than blame. By approaching issues collaboratively, you foster a problem-solving mindset that benefits the entire project. Implement a solution swiftly to prevent further delays once a solution is agreed upon. Whether it's redoing a section of drywall or adjusting a misaligned door frame, timely corrective actions ensure that quality is maintained throughout, leading to a finished barndominium that meets your standards.

If you are unable to visit the worksite as often as you'd like, cameras can be a useful tool in monitoring days/hours worked, delivery of materials and other items.

4.6 SAFETY FIRST: ESSENTIAL SAFETY PRACTICES

Safety is not just a priority; it's the foundation of every successful construction project. Developing a comprehensive safety plan at the project's start is crucial. Identify potential hazards and risks specific to your site, considering everything from machinery use to environmental factors. This plan acts as a guide, outlining protocols to minimize risks and protect everyone involved.

Enforcing strict safety protocols consistently is essential for maintaining high safety standards. Regularly review and update safety practices to reflect any changes in the worksite or regulations. This proactive approach not only reduces the likelihood of accidents but also demonstrates your commitment to safety excellence. When everyone knows and follows the protocols diligently, the worksite becomes a safer, more productive environment.

Preparing for emergencies is an integral part of your safety strategy. Ensure emergency contact information and the location of first aid supplies and equipment are clearly posted on-site. These preparations ensure that should an emergency arise, everyone knows what to do and where to go, minimizing confusion and ensuring a swift response. You create a worksite where quality craftsmanship can flourish without compromise by prioritizing safety at every stage.

TURNING DREAMS INTO REALITIES

"Dare to live the life you have dreamed for yourself. Go forward and make your dreams come true."

RALPH WALDO EMERSON

Many people dream of a family home that offers what a barndominium offers—even if the word itself is new to them. They dream of a home with space, character, and the opportunity to embrace comfort at the same time as personal expression. For many people, though, this remains an unattainable dream. They're overwhelmed by the challenges they fear will lie ahead and doubt their ability to see the project through from beginning to end. But, as you may remember from the introduction, I believe that everyone deserves to live the life they dream of, and I know that many more people would feel empowered to do this if only they had the right guidance from the beginning. My goal in writing this book was to help readers to turn their dream into an achievable goal, and I hope that by this stage in the book, you're excited about the possibilities of your own barndominium journey.

Excitement is inspiring, so I'd like to invite you to join me on my mission to help as many people as I can to move towards the lifestyle of their dreams—and the good news is that you can do this very easily by leaving a short review online.

By leaving a review of this book on Amazon, you'll inspire new readers to investigate the practicalities of a barndominium and start planning the home of their dreams.

Reviews help to connect books with the audiences they're intended for, and they also inspire people to take action on matters that might otherwise remain abstract ideas or unattainable dreams. With just a few minutes of your time, you could inspire a life-changing journey and help someone else to achieve their dream home.

Thank you so much for your support. I truly appreciate it.

Scan the QR code below

CHAPTER FIVE

CONSTRUCTION PHASE
FROM GROUNDBREAKING TO FINISH

The moment has arrived—standing on the land where your barndominium will soon rise. This is where dreams begin to take shape, and blueprints become foundations. The ground beneath your feet holds the promise of a home that will reflect your vision and lifestyle. Breaking ground is not merely a physical act; it's a symbolic step into your future. Every shovel of dirt, every measurement taken, sets the stage for what will become your sanctuary. Let's explore how to prepare this site thoroughly, ensuring that every aspect is ready for the construction journey ahead.

5.1 SITE ASSESSMENT AND PREPERATION

Conducting a thorough site assessment is crucial before any construction begins. This process involves evaluating several key factors that determine the suitability of your land for building. Soil testing is foundational, providing insights into soil stability and drainage capabilities. This information is vital as it influences the structural integrity of your future home. Without stable soil, the risk of shifting or settling increases, potentially compromising the building. Identifying potential environmental hazards, such as protected wildlife or contaminated land, can prevent costly legal issues and ensure compliance with local regulations. Understanding these elements early on sets the stage for a successful build, minimizing surprises that could derail progress.

Once the assessment is complete, it's time to plan for site preparation activities. Clearing the site of vegetation and debris is the first task. This may involve removing trees, shrubs, and any existing structures that could impede construction. Proper clearing provides a clean slate and ensures that no roots or debris will interfere with the foundation. Following clearing, grading the land becomes essential. Grading involves shaping the ground to facilitate proper drainage, preventing water accumulation that could harm the structure or lead to erosion. This step creates a level surface, providing a solid base for your barndominium and ensuring longevity.

Erosion control measures are vital during this phase to protect the integrity of your site. Installing silt fences and sediment traps is an effective strategy to prevent soil displacement caused by rain or wind. These barriers capture sediment, keeping it from washing away and protecting nearby water sources from contamination. Cover crops or mulch can also stabilize the soil, reducing erosion risks and promoting healthier soil conditions. These measures are environmentally responsible and protect your investment, keeping the land stable and ready for construction.

Facilitating construction access and utilities is the next critical step. Creating temporary access roads allows construction vehicles and equipment to reach the site efficiently, reducing delays and potential damage to the landscape. These roads must be planned carefully to handle the weight and frequency of construction traffic. Arranging for temporary water and electrical connections is also necessary to support the construction process. These utilities are essential for powering equipment and ensuring workers have the resources to complete the job safely and effectively. Setting these up early in the process ensures that work can proceed without interruptions, keeping the project on schedule.

Checklist: Site Preparation Essentials

- Conduct soil testing for stability and drainage.
- Evaluate environmental hazards and compliance requirements.
- Clear vegetation and debris from the site.
- Grade the land for proper drainage.
- Implement erosion control with silt fences and cover crops.
- Establish temporary access roads.
- Arrange for temporary water and electrical connections.

With these foundational steps in place, your site is prepared for the exciting construction phase ahead. These actions contribute to a smooth build and lay the groundwork for a barndominium that will stand the test of time.

5.2 FRAMING AND STRUCTURE: BUILDING THE SHELL

As you stand on the cleared and prepared land, it's time to focus on framing your barndominium. Choosing the right materials is crucial. Steel and wood are the primary contenders, each with its unique benefits. Steel framing is renowned for its strength and durability, offering a modern look and superior resistance to pests, fire, and moisture. It's particularly advantageous in areas prone to extreme weather, providing a robust framework that requires minimal maintenance.

On the other hand, wood framing offers traditional charm and versatility, easy customization, and excellent insulation properties. When considering these materials, reviewing their load-bearing capacities and how they align with your design vision is essential. Steel offers larger open spaces without interior columns, whereas wood provides warmth and a classic aesthetic. Consulting with an experienced builder will help you make an informed decision that fits your budget and lifestyle.

Once you've settled on the right materials, the framing process begins, marking a significant step in constructing your barndominium's structural framework. This phase involves erecting the walls and roof trusses, creating the skeleton of your home. Precision is key here, as accurate measurements ensure that everything aligns perfectly. The installation of support beams and columns follows, providing the necessary stability and strength. These elements form the backbone of your structure, supporting the weight of the roof and any additional loads. During this stage, it's vital to work with skilled professionals who understand the intricacies of framing. Their expertise ensures that the framework is functional and aesthetically pleasing, setting the stage for the next steps in your construction journey.

Ensuring the structural integrity of your barndominium is paramount as the framing progresses. Key inspections and tests are necessary to confirm that everything is stable and secure. Checking the alignment and level of structural components is critical to this process. Any discrepancies can lead to issues down the line, such as uneven floors or misaligned walls. Conducting load tests where applicable further verifies the framework's ability to support the intended loads. These tests simulate your barndominium's pressures, ensuring it can withstand daily use and environmental factors. Addressing these aspects early prevents potential problems and guarantees a safe, resilient home.

Incorporating design elements into the structure during framing adds character and functionality. Pre-installing window and door frames allow for seamless integration into the overall design, reducing the need for later adjustments. This foresight ensures that the architectural features align with the framing, creating a cohesive look. Additionally, consider allowing for future expansions or modifications. By planning for these possibilities during the framing stage, you provide flexibility for growth or changes in the future. This might involve leaving space for additional rooms or designing structural components that can accommodate new features. This approach enhances your barndominium's adaptability and adds long-term value to your investment.

5.3 ROOFING AND SIDING: CHOOSING THE RIGHT MATERIALS

Picking the right materials for your barndominium's exterior is a decision that impacts both aesthetics and durability. When it comes to roofing, metal stands out as a top contender. Its longevity and low maintenance requirements make it highly appealing. Metal roofs are known for their ability to withstand harsh weather conditions, from heavy snowfall to intense heat, providing a protective shield that ensures your home remains safe and dry. The sleek, modern look of metal roofing also adds a contemporary touch, making it a favorite for those seeking a modern aesthetic. Metal roofs are also notoriously noisy so additional insulation may be needed to negate the noise. However, if budget constraints are a major consideration, asphalt shingles offer a cost-effective alternative. They are versatile, coming in various colors and styles, allowing for customization to suit your personal taste. While they may require more maintenance than metal, asphalt shingles remain a popular choice due to their affordability and ease of installation.

Siding is another critical element of your barndominium's exterior, serving both protective and decorative purposes. Metal siding offers durability and a modern appeal that complements the sleek lines of a contemporary barndominium. It stands resilient against the elements, requiring minimal upkeep while providing a clean, polished look. Wood siding might be the way to go if you're drawn to a more traditional appearance. Its natural texture and warmth can give your barndominium a classic, rustic feel that resonates with the charm of country living. However, wood requires regular maintenance to prevent rot and insect damage, a factor that weighs against its aesthetic benefits. Both metal and wood have their pros and cons, and your choice will largely depend on the look you wish to achieve and the level of upkeep you're willing to commit to.

You can use almost any material for the exterior of a barndominium that you can use for a "regular" home, including stucco, board and batten, brick, stone, etc. However, many of the cost savings from building a barndominium come from the concept that the exterior consists of low-cost materials, such as metal siding.

The installation of roofing and siding demands precision to ensure they perform their protective roles effectively. Weatherproofing membranes and sealants are crucial in this process. They create a barrier against moisture, preventing leaks that could lead to structural damage over time. Proper alignment and overlap of materials are essential to achieving a seamless finish. This attention to detail enhances the visual appeal and ensures the structure's integrity, keeping the elements at bay. Skilled installation minimizes the risk of future repairs, providing peace of mind that your home is well-protected.

Insulation and ventilation are integral components of roofing and siding that should not be overlooked. Installing attic vents and ridge caps facilitates airflow, preventing the buildup of moisture and heat that can compromise the roof's longevity. These elements work together to maintain a balanced temperature within the home, reducing the strain on heating and cooling systems and enhancing energy efficiency. Choosing insulated siding adds an extra layer of protection, improving your home's thermal performance. This contributes to a comfortable indoor environment and reduces energy consumption, leading to long-term cost savings. The combination of effective insulation and ventilation ensures that your barndominium remains a comfortable and efficient space, adaptable to seasonal changes and varying weather conditions.

5.4 INTERIOR LAYOUT: WALLS, FLOORS, AND MORE

As you step inside the shell of your barndominium, the blank canvas of interior space awaits your creative touch. Planning for efficient space utilization is paramount in transforming this structure into a home that reflects your lifestyle and meets your needs. Designing multifunctional rooms can maximize the available space, ensuring every square foot serves a purpose. Open-concept layouts are particularly effective, allowing fluid movement and interaction across spaces. These layouts remove barriers, creating larger communal areas that encourage socializing and flexibility in how each room is used.

Selecting quality materials for your interiors is another crucial aspect of creating a durable and inviting environment. Flooring is one of the most significant considerations, as it impacts both aesthetics and functionality. Hardwood floors offer an elegant and timeless look, with the added benefits of durability and easy maintenance. They can suit various design styles, from rustic to modern. If budget constraints are a concern, laminate flooring provides a cost-effective alternative that mimics wood's appearance while offering wear-and-tear resilience.

Regarding walls, options like drywall and paneling offer versatility in design. Drywall is a practical choice for creating smooth surfaces ready for painting, while paneling can add texture and character to a room. Both materials provide a solid foundation for your interior decor, enabling you to personalize your space with finishes that align with your vision.

Coordinating utilities and fixtures within the interior layout requires careful planning to ensure functionality and convenience. Consider the layout of key areas like the kitchen and bathroom, where plumbing plays a vital role. Efficient plumbing layouts ensure that water and waste management systems function seamlessly, reducing the risk of future issues. Integrating these elements into your design not only streamlines the construction process but also enhances day-to-day living, providing a home that is as practical as it is beautiful.

Focusing on finishing touches can transform a simple structure into a warm and welcoming home. Installing trim and molding adds depth and elegance to your interior, framing walls and ceilings with a polished finish. These details create visual interest and a sense of completeness, elevating the overall aesthetic. Choosing paint colors and finishes is an opportunity to reflect your personal style. The right palette can influence the mood of a room, with soft neutrals creating a calming environment and bold hues injecting energy and personality. Consider the interplay of light and color, as natural light can alter how shades appear throughout the day. These finishing touches are the final strokes in your barndominium masterpiece, bringing together all the elements to create a cohesive and inviting space.

5.5 ENERGY EFFICIENCY: INCORPORATING GREEN TECHNOLOGIES

As you envision your barndominium, consider how it can be a model of energy efficiency and sustainability. Implementing energy-efficient systems is a smart move that benefits both your wallet and the environment. Start by installing solar panels and inverters, transforming sunlight into electricity to power your home. This renewable energy source reduces reliance on traditional power grids, leading to significant cost savings over time. Pairing solar panels with energy-efficient HVAC units further enhances this setup. These advanced systems effectively regulate your home's climate, using less energy to maintain comfort throughout the year. The initial investment in these technologies might be substantial, but the long-term savings and environmental impact make them worthwhile.

Enhancing insulation and sealing your barndominium is another crucial step in boosting thermal efficiency. Proper insulation is a barrier, keeping your home warm in winter and cool in summer. Consider applying spray foam or blown-in insulation, both of which fill gaps thoroughly and offer superior thermal performance. These materials help maintain a consistent indoor temperature, reducing the need for excessive heating or cooling. Additionally, sealing gaps and cracks is essential to prevent air leaks that can undermine insulation efforts. Even small openings around windows, doors, or electrical outlets can lead to energy loss, so meticulous sealing ensures that your home remains energy-efficient and comfortable.

Incorporating smart home technologies into your barndominium provides a modern edge in managing energy consumption. Smart thermostats for climate control allow you to adjust temperatures remotely, optimizing comfort while minimizing energy use. These devices learn your preferences over time, creating schedules that align with your daily routine and reduce unnecessary heating or cooling. Pairing this with energy monitoring systems offers a comprehensive view of your usage patterns. These systems track energy consumption, providing insights into where you can make adjustments for further savings. By understanding your energy habits better, you can make informed decisions that contribute to efficiency and sustainability.

Promoting sustainable water usage within your home is equally important. Installing low-flow fixtures and dual-flush toilets is a straightforward way to conserve water without sacrificing performance. These fixtures use less water for everyday tasks, significantly reducing your household's overall consumption. Consider rainwater harvesting systems for irrigation as well. These systems collect rainwater for use in watering gardens or landscaping, reducing dependency on municipal water supplies. By capturing and utilizing natural precipitation, you save water and lower your utility bills. Combining these techniques creates a barndominium that respects and preserves natural resources while providing a comfortable living environment.

Focusing on energy efficiency and sustainability in your barndominium is not just about adopting new technologies; it's about creating a home that aligns with your values and lifestyle. Each decision, from the insulation you choose to the smart systems you install, contributes to an eco-friendly and cost-effective space. The result is a home that meets your needs and sets a standard for responsible living. Through these choices, your barndominium becomes more than just a structure—it becomes a testament to thoughtful, sustainable living.

5.6 HANDLING DELAYS: WEATHER AND OTHER CHALLENGES

As you progress through your barndominium build, one thing becomes clear: nature doesn't always cooperate. Weather can throw a wrench into even the best-laid plans, so preparing for these potential delays is crucial. Understanding local weather patterns can help you schedule critical tasks around the seasons. For instance, avoid pouring concrete during the rainy season. Areas with low temperatures and high snowfall will have a shorter building season. Using weather-resistant materials and techniques also provides an extra layer of protection against unpredictable conditions, helping to mitigate damage and reduce setbacks. These proactive steps ensure that your project stays on track despite the whims of nature.

Beyond the weather, supply chain disruptions pose another significant challenge. Material shortages and delays can halt construction, leading to increased costs and frustration. To combat this, order materials well in advance. This approach provides a buffer against unexpected delays, ensuring that your project has the resources it needs when it needs them. Additionally, identifying alternative suppliers can be a lifesaver. If one source falls through, having a backup plan allows you to pivot quickly and keep moving forward. This flexibility is key in today's fluctuating market, where supply chain issues are increasingly common.

Labor shortages and scheduling conflicts are also hurdles that can disrupt your timeline. Building strong relationships with local contractors helps ensure you have the necessary workforce. Reliable contractors are more likely to prioritize your project if you've established a rapport and pay them on time as agreed. For contractors, cross-training workers to perform multiple tasks adds versatility to your crew. This approach allows you to reassign workers as needed, filling gaps and maintaining productivity. It's a strategic move that maximizes your resources and keeps the momentum going, even when faced with unexpected personnel issues.

Contingency planning is the final piece of the puzzle, providing a safety net for unforeseen challenges. Allocate additional time for critical project phases, recognizing that delays are often part of the construction process. This extra time helps absorb minor setbacks, preventing them from snowballing into major issues. Maintaining a flexible project timeline is equally important. Building in some leeway allows you to adjust schedules without derailing the entire project. This adaptability is vital in navigating the ups and downs of construction, ensuring that your barndominium progresses steadily toward completion.

Handling these challenges will lay a solid foundation for success. The construction phase can be unpredictable, but with careful planning and a proactive mindset, you can overcome obstacles and keep your project on track. As you move forward, these strategies will serve as a guide, helping you navigate the complexities of building a home that reflects your vision and meets your needs.

CHAPTER SIX

DESIGN AND DECOR
CREATING YOUR UNIQUE SPACE

Imagine walking into your barndominium for the first time. The walls echo with potential, waiting for your personal touch to transform them into a home. This is where your creativity takes center stage, and rustic chic design offers a perfect blend of old and new. This style captures the essence of rustic elegance while embracing modern simplicity, creating a harmonious balance that feels both timeless and fresh. It's like weaving together the threads of history with the fibers of contemporary life, producing a tapestry of comfort and style that is uniquely yours. The charm of rustic chic lies in its ability to blend the warmth of traditional materials with the sleek lines of modern design, offering a canvas where you can express individuality.

6.1 DEFINE YOUR STYLE: BALANCING OLD AND NEW

Color palettes and textures play a pivotal role in achieving rustic chic harmony. Earthy tones like deep greens, warm browns, and soft grays provide a neutral backdrop that enhances the natural beauty of your materials. These shades can be paired with metallic accents to add a touch of modernity. Picture a kitchen where brushed copper fixtures glimmer against a backdrop of slate tiles. This combination of colors and textures creates depth and interest, drawing the eye and inviting exploration. Mixing rough-hewn wood with smooth surfaces like polished concrete or glass adds another layer of sophistication. This balance of textures ensures your space feels thoughtfully curated, with every element contributing to the overall aesthetic.

Achieving a balance between old and new is key to mastering rustic chic style. Combining vintage finds with contemporary art offers a way to juxtapose different eras and influences. Consider a gallery wall where an abstract painting hangs beside a collection of antique mirrors. This eclectic mix highlights the uniqueness of each piece, creating a personalized and engaging display. Textiles play an important role in softening the harder edges of modern materials. Linen curtains and wool throws introduce warmth and texture, inviting touch and comfort. These fabrics drape naturally, enhancing the room's coziness without overpowering the design.

Reflection Exercise: Defining Your Rustic Chic Style

Take a moment to reflect on what rustic chic means to you. Consider the elements that resonate most—whether it's the warmth of wood, the gleam of metal, or the charm of vintage finds. Create a mood board, either digitally or physically, gathering images and samples that capture your vision. This exercise will help clarify your preferences and guide your design choices, ensuring your barndominium reflects your style and meets your needs.

6.2 OPEN-CONCEPT LIVING: MAXIMIZING SPACE

Open-concept living invites a sense of freedom into your home by allowing spaces to flow naturally into one another. This design strategy is about creating a functional environment without the obstruction of walls. To achieve this, define zones without physical barriers. Area rugs are excellent tools for delineating spaces. A plush rug under the dining table can subtly separate it from the living room area, while a different texture or color in the kitchen zone can provide visual cues about each space's function. This approach maintains an open feel while organizing your layout intuitively.

The placement of furniture in an open-concept space requires both creativity and practicality. Floating furniture arrangements can help maintain the open flow. Instead of pushing all your pieces against the walls, consider placing a sofa or chairs in the middle of the room. This setup encourages movement around the furniture, reinforcing the open concept. Multi-functional furniture, like modular sofas, offers flexibility in how you use your space. These pieces can be rearranged easily to accommodate different activities or gatherings. For instance, a sectional sofa can be split into individual seating when hosting guests or reconfigured into a cozy nook for family movie nights. This adaptability ensures that your living space can evolve with your needs, providing comfort and efficiency.

Lighting plays a crucial role in enhancing the openness of your space. Well-placed lighting can highlight different areas without interrupting the flow. Pendant lights can define the dining area, drawing attention to it as a focal point without isolating it visually from other areas. These fixtures can add elegance and style, complementing the overall design theme. Recessed lighting offers unobtrusive illumination, keeping the ceiling clean and uncluttered. This type of lighting provides general illumination without casting shadows that might break up the space. By using a combination of these lighting strategies, you can create a warm and inviting atmosphere that enhances the functionality and aesthetics of your open-concept home.

Managing acoustics and privacy in open layouts requires thoughtful solutions to maintain comfort without sacrificing openness. Acoustic panels or fabric wall hangings can significantly reduce noise, making conversations clearer and reducing echo. These elements can be strategically placed in areas where sound tends to bounce, such as high ceilings or long walls. They come in various designs and colors, allowing you to incorporate them into your decor continuously. Bookshelves or screens can serve a dual purpose, providing visual breaks and additional privacy without erecting permanent walls. These additions can create intimate nooks for reading or working, offering a sense of separation when needed. Addressing acoustics and privacy ensures that your open-concept space remains functional and comfortable without compromising its airy feel.

6.3 LOFT LIVING: UTILIZING VERTICAL SPACE

In a barndominium, every square inch matters, and vertical space is a treasure trove of possibilities. Picture this: your main living area flows effortlessly, but there lies untapped potential above. This is where lofts come into play. Installing a loft can dramatically increase your available space, providing a cozy retreat or a practical storage solution. Imagine a lofted bedroom that offers privacy while maintaining an open feel. It's a sanctuary perched above the hustle and bustle, perfect for unwinding. Beneath it, you might find a snug reading nook or a hidden storage area, cleverly maximizing the space beneath the loft. Tall shelving units can line the walls, reach up to the ceiling, hold everything from books to decorative items, and use the vertical dimension without encroaching on the floor area below.

Creating a functional loft design combines practicality with style. A lofted bedroom, for instance, can incorporate built-in storage solutions like drawers or shelves under the bed platform. This not only saves space but also keeps the area tidy and organized.

A loft can transform into a secluded office for those working from home. Equip it with a space-saving desk that folds away when not in use. This setup provides a dedicated workspace while allowing the area to function as an additional guest room or hobby zone when needed. The key is to design with versatility in mind, ensuring each element can serve multiple purposes without sacrificing comfort or aesthetics.

Safety and accessibility are paramount when designing lofts. Sturdy railings are necessary, providing a secure barrier without obstructing views or light. Choose materials that complement your overall design—perhaps sleek metal for a modern look or warm wood for a more traditional feel. Stair designs should prioritize both safety and aesthetics. Spiral staircases offer a compact, stylish solution, while traditional stairs can double as storage with built-in drawers in the risers. Ladders, too, can be an option, especially for spaces used less frequently. Ensure they are robust and easy to navigate, with non-slip steps and handrails for added safety.

Aesthetic elements elevate a loft from a mere functional space to a design feature. Exposed beams can add architectural interest, drawing the eye upward and emphasizing the height of the space. These beams can be left in their natural wood state for a rustic touch or painted to match the room's color scheme for a more cohesive look. Skylights are another transformative addition, flooding the loft with natural light and creating a sense of openness. They offer a view of the sky, bringing the outside in and enhancing the loft's appeal. Imagine lying in your lofted bedroom, watching the stars through a skylight, or enjoying the morning sun as it streams in. These elements not only enhance the loft's functionality but also contribute to the overall ambiance of your barndominium, making it a beautiful and practical space.

6.4 PERSONALIZING YOUR SPACE: CUSTOMIZATION IDEAS

Personalizing your barndominium goes beyond mere decoration; it's about infusing your essence into every corner, making your home a true reflection of who you are. This is where self-expression takes center stage. Displaying personal collections or art pieces can transform a space, turning blank walls into a gallery that narrates your story. Imagine a cozy nook adorned with your favorite paintings or photographs, each piece adding warmth and character to the room. These elements enhance the aesthetic appeal and create a space that's uniquely yours, where each glance offers a glimpse into your passions and memories.

Customization offers endless possibilities. Consider the cabinetry or built-ins in your home as canvases for creativity. Customizing these features allows you to tailor them to your specific needs, whether a kitchen caters to your culinary adventures or a library wall that houses your cherished book collection. This level of personalization optimizes functionality and adds a layer of sophistication and exclusivity to your home. The beauty of custom-built pieces lies in their ability to seamlessly integrate with existing structures while standing out as focal points that draw admiration.

Exploring unique design elements further enhances the customization process. Statement walls, for instance, present an opportunity to infuse boldness into your decor. Whether through vibrant colors or intricate patterns, these walls can serve as striking backdrops that energize a room. They invite creativity, encouraging you to experiment with textures and finishes that reflect your style. Themed rooms offer another avenue for distinctiveness, allowing you to dedicate spaces to specific interests or activities. Perhaps a room dedicated to music, complete with instruments and memorabilia, or a tranquil meditation space with calming colors and soft lighting. These thematic choices transform rooms into immersive experiences tailored to your lifestyle.

The allure of bespoke furniture and fixtures cannot be overstated. Commissioning a custom dining table ensures the perfect fit for your space and provides a centerpiece that sparks conversation. These pieces are crafted with your vision in mind, resulting in furniture that aligns perfectly with your aesthetic preferences and functional needs. Handmade light fixtures or hardware add another layer of personalization, offering unique touches that elevate your decor. These elements, meticulously crafted to your specifications, enrich your home with character and distinction, ensuring that every detail harmonizes with your overall design concept.

Incorporating sentimental items into your decor adds depth and meaning to your space. When displayed thoughtfully, family heirlooms serve as powerful focal points that honor your heritage. Whether it's an antique clock that has ticked through generations or a cherished quilt that has warmed many a winter night, these pieces tell stories that connect past and present. Photographs and memorabilia can be artfully arranged in gallery walls, creating a tapestry of memories that evoke emotion and nostalgia. These personal touches enhance the visual appeal and infuse your home with a sense of identity and belonging, making it a sanctuary that resonates with warmth and familiarity.

Call to Action: Crafting Your Personalized Space

Take a moment to reflect on the elements that define your style. Consider incorporating personal collections, unique design features, and bespoke elements into your barndominium. Sketch out ideas or create a mood board to visualize your thoughts. This exercise will guide you in crafting a space that truly reflects your personality and preferences, ensuring your barndominium is a home that feels authentically yours.

6.5 INCORPORATING SMART HOME TECHNOLOGIES

Imagine transforming your barndominium into a space that reflects your style and anticipates your needs. This is where smart home technologies come into play, offering a blend of convenience and innovation that elevates everyday living. At the heart of smart home systems are automation features that manage lighting and climate control with precision and ease. Picture entering a room where lights adjust to your presence or a thermostat that learns your schedule, ensuring your home is always at the perfect temperature.

Selecting the right devices to complement your lifestyle is key. Smart speakers and assistants, like Amazon Echo or Google Nest, serve as central hubs for your smart home, allowing you to control various elements with simple voice commands. These devices can play music, answer questions, and even control other smart gadgets, bringing a new level of interaction to your daily routine.

Integrating technology into your decor can be easy, ensuring your home remains aesthetically pleasing while embracing modern conveniences. Concealing wires and devices is a practical first step. Consider running cables through walls or behind baseboards to keep them out of sight, maintaining the clean lines of your interior design. Smart bulbs fit easily into existing fixtures, providing the benefits of smart lighting without requiring major changes. These bulbs can be controlled remotely, allowing you to adjust brightness or color to suit the mood, all while preserving the look of your favorite lamps and chandeliers. This thoughtful integration ensures that technology enhances rather than detracts from the beauty of your home.

The true magic of smart home technology lies in the convenience and efficiency it brings to everyday life. Voice-activated controls mean you can manage your home's functions hands-free, whether it's turning off the lights as you leave a room or adjusting the thermostat without getting up from the couch. Automated schedules further enhance this convenience, allowing you to set routines that align with your lifestyle. Imagine waking up to a home where the blinds open automatically, letting in the morning sun, or returning in the evening to a warmly lit living room that welcomes you home. These features simplify daily tasks and create a more personalized and responsive living environment, enhancing both comfort and functionality.

6.6 SUSTAINABLE DECOR: ECO-FRIENDLY CHOICES

In today's world, choosing eco-friendly decor is more than a trend; it's necessary. It's about making choices that benefit our planet while enhancing our living spaces. By opting for sustainable decor, you reduce your carbon footprint significantly. This means less energy consumption during production and fewer pollutants released into the atmosphere. Supporting sustainable industries is another crucial aspect. Buying products made from recycled or responsibly sourced materials encourages businesses to prioritize environmental stewardship. This helps preserve natural resources and fosters innovation in eco-friendly manufacturing practices. These choices contribute to a healthier planet, ensuring that your home's beauty doesn't come at the expense of the earth.

Selecting the right materials plays a pivotal role in creating a sustainable home. Furniture made from reclaimed wood is a prime example. These pieces not only have a unique character, with each imperfection telling a story, but they also prevent further deforestation. When choosing textiles for upholstery and drapery, consider organic options. Organic cotton, linen, or hemp are grown without harmful pesticides and chemicals, making them safer for the environment and your home. These textiles offer durability and style, proving that you don't have to sacrifice aesthetics for sustainability. By choosing these materials, you create an environmentally conscious and visually appealing home.

Incorporating plants and natural elements into your decor brings numerous benefits. Indoor plants, for example, enhance a room's visual appeal and purify the air. They absorb toxins and release oxygen, making the air healthier to breathe. Consider adding a variety of plants, like ferns or succulents, to different parts of your home to create a vibrant and lively atmosphere. Natural fiber rugs and baskets can also add warmth and texture to your decor. Made from materials like jute or sisal, these items are biodegradable and often produced sustainably, making them a perfect addition to an eco-friendly home. These elements connect your living space to nature, creating a calming and inviting environment.

Upcycling and repurposing materials is a creative way to reduce waste and personalize your home. Consider undertaking DIY projects using salvaged materials. You may have an old piece of furniture that could be sanded down and refinished, transforming it into a unique centerpiece for your living room. Reimagining old furniture with new finishes saves money and gives you a sense of accomplishment. This approach encourages resourcefulness and creativity, turning potential waste into cherished items. It's about seeing the potential in what others might discard and creating something beautiful and functional from it. This mindset benefits the environment and adds a personal touch to your decor, ensuring your home is filled with pieces that hold meaning and history.

Visual Element: Eco-Friendly Decor Checklist

Consider creating a checklist to guide your sustainable decor choices. Include items like reclaimed wood furniture, organic textiles, and upcycled projects. Use this list as a reference when shopping or planning your decor to ensure your home remains eco-friendly and aligned with your values.

As you integrate sustainable decor into your home, remember that each choice contributes to a more significant movement toward environmental responsibility. Your house becomes a testament to what is possible when creativity meets consciousness. By focusing on eco-friendly choices, you create a space that is not only beautiful but also sustainable, setting a foundation for a more responsible way of living. With these principles in mind, you're ready to explore how these ideas seamlessly blend with your lifestyle, enhancing your home and your impact on the world.

CHAPTER SEVEN

SETTLING IN
TRANSITIONING TO BARNDOMINIUM LIVING

Stepping into your new barndominium is like opening the first page of an unwritten chapter in your life. The space echoes with potential, ready to be shaped into a home that reflects your values and aspirations. Here, the concept of minimalism finds its perfect match. In the vast openness of a barndominium, embracing minimalism can transform the living experience, offering a sanctuary from the clutter and chaos of the outside world. This lifestyle isn't just about reducing possessions; it's about cultivating an environment where simplicity reigns, allowing you to focus on what truly matters.

7.1 EMBRACE MINIMALISM: A NEW WAY OF LIVING

The heart of minimalism lies in its ability to reduce clutter and focus on essentials. In a barndominium, this approach enhances the expansive feel of the space, making it both functional and calming. By stripping back to the essentials, you create an environment that fosters mental clarity and focus. Imagine waking up to a room that breathes with space, where every item has its place and purpose. This clarity extends beyond physical surroundings, encouraging a mindset that values intention over accumulation. It's about living with less but experiencing more, savoring the freedom that comes with owning only what serves a purpose or brings joy.

Decluttering is an essential first step in embracing this lifestyle. Begin by sorting your possessions into three categories: keep, donate, and discard. This process encourages a deep reflection on what truly adds value to your life. As you sift through your belongings, ask yourself if each item serves a purpose or holds sentimental value. Letting go of what doesn't align with your vision frees up physical and mental space. Utilize storage solutions for essential items to keep your living area organized and tidy. Consider custom built-in storage solutions that efficiently use available space and blend seamlessly with your home's architecture, maintaining the minimalist aesthetic while ensuring functionality.

Intentional living is at the core of minimalism. It's about making mindful choices about your possessions and how you spend your time and energy. Prioritize quality over quantity, choosing well-made and long-lasting items rather than disposable. This philosophy extends to every aspect of life, fostering a deeper connection with nature and your surroundings. Imagine spending time outdoors, gardening, or simply enjoying the natural beauty around your barndominium. These moments of connection remind you of the simple pleasures in life, grounding you in a lifestyle that values experiences over material possessions.

Achieving a minimalist aesthetic in your barndominium involves careful design choices. Use neutral color palettes and simple decor to create a serene and cohesive environment. Soft whites, gentle grays, and earthy tones work together to expand the sense of space, making rooms feel larger and more inviting. Incorporate multifunctional furniture pieces that enhance versatility without sacrificing style. A sofa bed or a wall-mounted desk can transform a room from a living area to a guest room or office, maximizing the use of space without adding clutter. These pieces serve multiple purposes and contribute to the clean, uncluttered look that defines minimalism.

Reflection Exercise: Embracing Minimalism

Take a moment to reflect on your personal journey towards minimalism. Consider the areas in your home and life where simplification could bring clarity and peace. What possessions could you live without? How might reducing clutter enhance your daily experience? Write down your thoughts and create a plan for incorporating minimalist principles into your barndominium.

Minimalism in a barndominium setting is not just a design choice; it's a way of living that prioritizes what truly matters. By embracing this lifestyle, you create a home that reflects your values, offering a space that is not only beautiful but also deeply aligned with your vision for a simpler, more intentional life.

7.2 BUILDING COMMUNITY: CONNECTING WITH NEIGHBORS

Transitioning to a barndominium lifestyle often means moving to a rural or semi-rural area, where the sense of community can be comforting and vital. The bonds you form with your neighbors can transform your experience, offering both support and camaraderie. In these settings, neighbors become more than just people living nearby. They become a network of support, sharing resources, experiences, and sometimes even meals. This camaraderie is especially valuable in rural areas, where services and amenities are spread further apart. When you know your neighbors, you have allies close by, ready to lend a hand or share a tool, which fosters a sense of belonging and security.

Participating actively in community life opens doors to shared resources and activities that enrich your living experience. Local clubs or organizations often serve as the heartbeat of rural communities. Whether it's a gardening club, a book group, or a volunteer organization, these groups provide opportunities to connect with others who share your interests. Being part of such circles allows you to contribute to and benefit from the community's wealth of knowledge and resources. Community events and gatherings—be they seasonal fairs, farmers' markets, or local festivals—are perfect venues to meet neighbors and forge new friendships. These events are not just social occasions but also platforms for collaboration and mutual support, enriching both personal lives and the community as a whole.

Fostering neighborly relationships can begin with simple gestures. Hosting informal meet-and-greets, like a backyard barbecue or a potluck dinner, invites casual interactions that can blossom into deeper connections. Such gatherings provide a relaxed setting where people feel comfortable sharing stories and experiences, laying the foundation for lasting friendships. Offering to help with local initiatives or projects is another way to build goodwill and rapport. Whether volunteering for a community cleanup or helping organize a local event, your involvement shows commitment and opens up channels of communication and cooperation.

In today's digital age, leveraging online platforms can enhance your connection to local and broader barndominium communities. Participating in online forums or social media groups dedicated to barndominium living offers a wealth of shared experiences and advice. These platforms connect you with enthusiasts from all over, providing insights and solutions you might not find locally. Sharing your experiences and advice contributes to the community and reinforces your sense of identity and belonging. Engaging with these online communities can be as rewarding as face-to-face interactions, offering support and camaraderie no matter the distance.

Community Building Exercise: Mapping Your Community

Create a map of your local area, marking the locations of neighbors, community centers, and local organizations. Use this map to identify opportunities for engagement and interaction. Consider how you can contribute to your community and what resources you might share or seek. This exercise helps visualize your community network, encouraging proactive involvement and strengthening connections.

Building a community in your new barndominium involves more than just living in a neighborhood. It's about actively participating, contributing, and reaping the benefits of shared experiences and resources. These connections enrich your life and provide a support network that enhances your well-being and community vitality.

7.3 OFF-GRID LIVING: BECOMING SELF-SUFFICIENT

Imagine stepping outside your barndominium, knowing that every bit of energy powering your home comes from the sun or wind, and every drop of water you use is collected and filtered by systems you've set up. Off-grid living is about independence from public utilities, a lifestyle choice emphasizing self-sufficiency and a deep connection to the natural world. It involves not relying on the grid for energy, water, or waste management but creating a self-sustaining environment that meets all your needs. Utilizing renewable energy sources is at the heart of this lifestyle.

Managing waste and water systems is an integral aspect of off-grid living. Rather than relying on municipal services, off-grid homes often use decentralized systems for water and waste. A rainwater collection system effectively captures natural water resources, reducing dependence on public water supplies. Rainwater collected from roofs can be stored in tanks, filtered, and used for irrigation, flushing toilets, or even drinking after appropriate treatment. Composting toilets or septic systems can handle waste sustainably, breaking down organic matter without the need for extensive plumbing infrastructure. These systems align with sustainability and resource conservation principles, allowing you to live in harmony with the environment.

Transitioning to self-sufficiency requires careful planning and gradual implementation. Begin by assessing your energy needs and installing solar panels accordingly. Consider the size and layout of your roof to maximize solar exposure, and choose panels that meet your power requirements. Battery storage is equally important, providing a buffer during times when the sun is low. Setting up a rainwater collection system can start small, with basic gutter and tank setups, expanding over time as you learn what best suits your needs. The process of becoming self-sufficient also involves cultivating a mindset of resourcefulness and learning to manage systems independently.

Sustainable food production is another exciting frontier in off-grid living. Growing your own food reduces reliance on store-bought produce and enhances your connection to the land. Starting a vegetable garden can be as simple or as elaborate as you desire, from a few raised beds to a fully-fledged greenhouse that extends the growing season. Consider the crops that thrive in your climate and soil type, and experiment with organic gardening methods. Raising chickens or other small livestock provides fresh eggs or meat, and they contribute to a closed-loop system where waste becomes fertilizer, enriching the soil for future crops. These practices ensure a steady food supply and foster a sense of accomplishment and sustainability.

Of course, off-grid living presents its own challenges, but each is an opportunity for learning and adaptation. Maintaining energy systems during cloudy seasons requires a robust setup and a backup generator for prolonged periods of low sunlight. Monitoring energy usage closely and adjusting habits to conserve power when necessary is essential—ensuring a reliable water supply year-round demands careful planning and perhaps multiple sources, like wells or additional rainwater tanks, especially in areas with variable rainfall. These challenges teach resilience and adaptability, equipping you with the skills to troubleshoot and improve your systems over time.

By embracing off-grid living, you not only reduce your environmental footprint but also gain a profound sense of independence and self-reliance. This lifestyle fosters a deeper appreciation for natural resources and encourages a harmonious relationship with the environment. As you progress, you'll find that each step towards self-sufficiency brings with it a greater understanding of the delicate balance of nature and the rewarding experience of living sustainably.

7.4 MAINTAINING YOUR BARNDOMINIUM: TIPS AND TRICKS

As you settle into your barndominium, it's important to establish a maintenance routine that keeps your home in top condition. Seasonal inspections and repairs are the backbone of this routine, ensuring that your barndominium withstands the elements and remains a safe, comfortable place to live. Begin with a thorough inspection of your property with each change of season. Look for any signs of wear or damage that may have occurred over the past months. Pay special attention to the condition of your roof and siding, as these are your first lines of defense against weather. Check for loose shingles, signs of leaks, or any areas where the siding may have become compromised. Promptly addressing these issues can prevent small problems from escalating into costly repairs. Cleaning gutters and downspouts is another crucial task, particularly in autumn when leaves can accumulate and block water flow. This helps ensure that water is directed away from the foundation, reducing the risk of water damage and maintaining the integrity of your home.

Preventative maintenance goes hand in hand with regular upkeep, emphasizing the need to address issues before they become major concerns. Regular servicing of HVAC systems and plumbing is essential. Schedule annual checks with professionals to ensure that these systems operate efficiently and catch any potential issues early. An HVAC system that runs smoothly prolongs its lifespan, enhances your comfort, and reduces energy costs. Similarly, checking plumbing systems can prevent leaks and water wastage. Inspect pipes regularly for any signs of deterioration or moisture and replace worn-out seals or joints as needed. These proactive steps safeguard your home against unexpected breakdowns and preserve the investment you've made in your barndominium.

Many maintenance tasks require professional expertise, but there are several simple tasks you can tackle yourself, saving time and money. Changing air filters in your HVAC system is one such task that can be done regularly to improve air quality and system efficiency. A clean filter allows for better airflow, making your home more comfortable while reducing energy costs. Replacing light bulbs and touching up paint are straightforward tasks that enhance your home's appearance and functionality. Keep an eye out for areas where paint may have chipped or faded, and apply fresh coats to maintain a polished look. Additionally, caulking around windows and doors helps seal any gaps that could lead to drafts or moisture intrusion. This improves energy efficiency and protects against potential water damage, which is especially important in maintaining the longevity of your barndominium.

Knowing when to call in professionals is a critical aspect of home maintenance. Licensed experts should always handle major electrical or plumbing issues to ensure safety and compliance with regulations. Attempting to fix these problems without proper knowledge can lead to dangerous situations or further damage. Structural repairs or modifications also fall into this category. If you notice any signs of structural weakness, such as cracks in the foundation or sagging beams, it's vital to consult with a professional immediately. They can assess the situation accurately and recommend the best course of action, preserving the integrity of your home and preventing further damage.

Maintenance Checklist: Keep Your Barndominium in Top Shape

- Inspect the roof and siding for damage and perform necessary repairs.
- Clean gutters and downspouts to ensure proper drainage.

- Service HVAC and plumbing systems annually, checking for leaks and inefficiencies.
- Change air filters regularly to maintain air quality.
- Touch up paint and caulk around windows and doors as needed.
- Consult professionals for major electrical, plumbing, or structural issues.

By following a regular maintenance routine and knowing when to seek professional help, you can keep your barndominium in excellent condition. This proactive approach protects your investment and ensures a safe and comfortable living environment for years to come.

7.5 PLANNING FOR FUTURE EXPANSION: ROOM TO GROW

When you first settle into your barndominium, it might seem like you've found your forever home ideally suited to your needs. Yet, life has a way of evolving, bringing changes that can alter what you require from your living space. Whether it's the joy of welcoming new family members, pursuing a home-based business, or simply desiring more space to breathe and grow, planning for these possibilities is important. Thinking ahead allows you to design a home that can adapt to your life. Consider the future as you lay the foundation for your barndominium, not just in a metaphorical sense but through tangible design choices that make expansion feasible and less disruptive.

Flexible design is key to accommodating potential changes. You might start by creating multi-use spaces that can serve different functions as needed. A room initially used as a guest bedroom could easily transform into an office or a playroom with a few adjustments. This adaptability ensures your home remains functional and relevant, regardless of how your needs change over time. Consider pre-planning for additional rooms or extensions during the initial design phase. You make future projects more straightforward by integrating structural elements that facilitate expansion, such as reinforced walls or adaptable layouts. This foresight saves time and money and minimizes the disruption of daily life when the time comes to expand.

Understanding local zoning regulations and securing the necessary permits are crucial steps in planning for expansion. Each region has its own rules regarding property development, and it's essential to familiarize yourself with them early on. This knowledge helps you plan effectively and ensures compliance, avoiding legal headaches down the line. When you're ready to expand, obtaining the proper permits is necessary to ensure your project aligns with local building codes and standards. This process involves submitting detailed plans for approval, which may require adjustments based on feedback from local authorities.

Stories from those who've successfully expanded their barndominiums highlight the possibilities and inspire new ideas. Take, for example, a couple who originally built a modest two-bedroom barndominium. As their family grew, they skillfully added a new wing, incorporating a spacious playroom and additional bedrooms without compromising the home's original charm. Another homeowner transformed unused attic space into a bright, airy studio for their burgeoning home business, proving that expansion doesn't always require building outward. These examples demonstrate that with creativity and planning, a barndominium can evolve to meet the changing needs of its residents.

The potential to expand your barndominium offers both freedom and flexibility. By planning ahead, you ensure your home can grow with you, adapting to life's changes gracefully and effortlessly. As you consider your own future needs, let these stories and strategies guide you, inspiring a vision of a home that serves your present and anticipates and embraces tomorrow's opportunities.

CHAPTER EIGHT

REALIZING THE DREAM
SUCCESS STORIES AND FUTURE TRENDS

Imagine a young couple standing on a plot of land that stretches into the horizon, the morning sun casting a warm glow over their future home site. They decided to leave the crowded city behind, seeking a life where they could connect with nature and each other more deeply. This couple embarked on a journey to build a sustainable barndominium nestled in the countryside, where fresh air and open spaces abound. Their vision included solar panels to harness the sun's energy, a rainwater collection system for sustainable water use, and a thriving vegetable garden that would provide fresh produce year-round. This dream was about creating a home and crafting a lifestyle centered around sustainability, simplicity, and self-sufficiency.

8.1 BARNDO LIVING: WHAT WILL THAT MEAN TO YOU

In a bustling urban area, an entrepreneur saw an opportunity to rethink traditional workspaces. Instead of a conventional office, they envisioned a barndominium that would serve as both a home and a creative business hub. This multipurpose environment included a spacious open-plan living area transitioning into a professional workspace. High ceilings and large windows brought in ample natural light, creating an inspiring setting for living and working. Using local materials added a layer of authenticity and connection to the community, while innovative design elements like indoor gardens and flexible workstations maximized the use of space. This setup enabled the entrepreneur to balance personal and professional life effectively, reducing commute times and enhancing productivity.

These stories are just the beginning. Across the country, individuals are discovering the unique benefits of barndominium living. In rural Pennsylvania, another family took on the challenge of transforming a dilapidated barn into a vibrant family retreat. They maintained the rustic exterior, preserving the historical character of the building while incorporating modern amenities inside. The result was a multi-level home that offered separate living quarters for family members, a gourmet kitchen for culinary adventures, and a cozy entertainment area for gatherings. The craftsmanship was evident in every detail, from the reclaimed wood used in the beams to the handcrafted cabinetry in the kitchen, creating a functional and beautifully unique space.

The impact of these projects on the homeowners' quality of life is profound. For the young couple in the countryside, the shift to sustainable living meant reduced utility bills and a greater sense of independence. They found joy in growing their own food and knowing their home minimized its impact on the environment. The entrepreneur experienced a newfound work-life balance, with the ability to transition between work and personal time seamlessly. This setup fostered a deeper connection with their community, as the barndominium became a hub for networking and creativity. For the family in Pennsylvania, the barndominium became a sanctuary where they could gather, play, and recharge, strengthening their bonds and enhancing their quality of life.

The reflections of these homeowners offer valuable insights for anyone considering a barndominium. One couple shared, "We faced challenges, but each one taught us something new about ourselves and what we truly value." Their advice to potential builders is to embrace the process and stay true to their vision. Another homeowner emphasized the importance of patience and persistence, noting, "There were times when we doubted our decisions, but seeing our completed home reminded us why we started." These testimonials highlight the resilience and creativity required to turn a dream into reality, offering encouragement to those on a similar path.

Reflection Activity: Envisioning Your Success Story

Take a moment to visualize your ideal barndominium. What lifestyle changes do you hope to achieve? Reflect on the lessons from these success stories and consider how to incorporate similar elements into your project. Write down your thoughts and aspirations, using them as a guiding star as you move forward in your barndominium journey.

8.2 OVERCOMING CHALLENGES: LESSONS FROM BARNDOMINIUM OWNERS

Building a barndominium presents a unique set of challenges, often starting with navigating complex zoning laws. Many first-time builders find themselves engulfed in a sea of regulations, unsure of where to begin. Zoning laws can vary significantly from one region to another, dictating what can be built and where. Understanding these laws is crucial, as they can impact everything from the size of your barndominium to the materials you can use. It's not uncommon for homeowners to encounter unexpected restrictions, leading to frustrating delays. This challenge is compounded by managing project timelines and budgets. Building a home is a significant financial undertaking, and staying on budget can be difficult when unforeseen expenses arise. Delays, whether due to weather, supply chain issues, or legal hurdles, can extend timelines and increase costs, putting additional strain on resources.

Experienced homeowners offer a wealth of strategies for overcoming these obstacles, starting with creative financing options. Some have turned to unconventional methods such as crowdfunding or securing loans through community banks that understand the unique nature of barndominium projects. Others have found success in negotiating payment plans with contractors, spreading costs over a longer period to ease financial pressure. Effective project management techniques are also key to staying on schedule. Many recommend breaking the project down into smaller, manageable phases, each with its own timeline and budget. This approach allows for flexibility and easier adjustments when needed. Regular check-ins with contractors and suppliers ensure everyone is aligned and potential issues are addressed promptly. By maintaining clear communication and setting realistic expectations, homeowners can navigate the complexities of construction more smoothly.

Adaptability and resilience are vital traits for anyone undertaking a barndominium project. Unforeseen issues are inevitable, whether they come in the form of design changes, budget constraints, or external factors like market fluctuations. Adjusting design plans in response to these challenges is often necessary. Some homeowners have had to scale back their original visions, opting for simpler designs or more cost-effective materials. Others have embraced the opportunity to innovate, finding creative solutions that enhance their homes in unexpected ways. Maintaining motivation through community support is another critical element. Engaging with local barndominium groups or online forums can provide encouragement and practical advice. Sharing experiences and learning from others who have faced similar challenges fosters a sense of camaraderie and determination.

Learning from mistakes is an invaluable part of the barndominium building experience. Many homeowners find that reflecting on their projects helps identify areas for improvement. Analyzing what could have been done differently provides insights to prevent future missteps. For instance, some realize that more thorough research into zoning laws could have saved time and resources. Others discover that better communication with contractors might have averted costly misunderstandings. Sharing these lessons with the wider community benefits everyone involved. By openly discussing successes and setbacks, homeowners contribute to a collective pool of knowledge that strengthens the barndominium community.

Reflection Prompt: Analyzing Your Journey

Consider the challenges you anticipate facing in your barndominium project. Reflect on past experiences where you overcame obstacles, and consider how those lessons can be applied here.

Use this exercise to prepare for the road ahead and write down potential strategies and resources you might need.

8.3 EMERGING TRENDS: WHAT'S NEXT FOR BARNDOMINIUMS?

In the evolving landscape of barndominium design, new trends are emerging that promise to redefine what these homes can offer. One significant trend is the integration of biophilic design elements, which aim to connect residents more closely with nature. This involves incorporating natural light, organic materials, and indoor plants to create spaces that promote well-being and tranquility. Imagine a living room with large windows that frame a view of the surrounding landscape, allowing sunlight to pour in and plants to thrive indoors. This design trend not only enhances the aesthetic appeal of barndominiums but also brings the calming effects of nature into everyday life, fostering a healthier living environment.

Sustainability continues to be a driving force in the barndominium industry, with advancements in technology paving the way for more eco-friendly homes. Advanced energy storage systems, such as high-efficiency batteries, are becoming commonplace, allowing homeowners to store renewable energy generated from solar panels or wind turbines. These systems ensure a steady energy supply even when natural conditions fluctuate, enhancing the sustainability of the home. Zero-waste building practices are also being implemented, focusing on reducing construction waste and recycling materials whenever possible. This shift towards sustainability reduces the environmental impact of building a barndominium and aligns with growing consumer demand for eco-conscious living solutions.

As we examine demographic shifts, it's clear that barndominiums attract a diverse range of homeowners. Younger generations, particularly millennials, are drawn to the affordability and customization options that barndominiums offer. They appreciate the opportunity to create unique spaces that reflect their values and lifestyle choices. Meanwhile, retirees increasingly seek low-maintenance, adaptable homes that allow them to age in place comfortably. Barndominiums, with their single-level designs and potential for accessibility modifications, are an ideal choice for this demographic. These shifts in who is choosing barndominium living highlight this housing option's versatility and broad appeal.

Looking ahead, the barndominium market is poised for expansion into urban areas, driven by innovative designs that blend traditional barn aesthetics with modern urban sensibilities. This urban expansion will likely include multi-use spaces that accommodate residential and commercial needs, making barndominiums a viable option for city dwellers seeking a unique living experience. Moreover, the demand for eco-friendly and smart homes is expected to rise as more people prioritize sustainability and technological integration in their living environments. With advancements in smart home technology, including automated systems for energy management and security, barndominiums will continue to evolve, offering cutting-edge solutions that meet the needs of future generations.

8.4 THE ROLE OF TECHNOLOGY IN FUTURE BUILDS

As we venture into the future of barndominium construction, technology stands at the forefront, reshaping how these unique homes are built and experienced. One of the most exciting developments is the use of 3D printing for structural components. This technology allows for the precise creation of complex parts that were once difficult or impossible to produce using traditional methods. Imagine designing intricate architectural details or custom features with the click of a button. The possibilities are endless, and the precision of 3D printing ensures that every element fits perfectly into your barndominium's design. Additionally, this method can reduce waste and lower costs, making it an attractive option for environmentally conscious builders.

Drones are another technological marvel making waves in the construction industry. These flying devices are revolutionizing site surveys and monitoring, providing builders with real-time data and insights. By capturing aerial views, drones can map out land with incredible accuracy, identifying potential issues before they become costly problems. They also monitor progress throughout construction, ensuring that every phase aligns with plans and timelines. This technology enhances efficiency and improves safety by reducing the need for workers to access hazardous areas. With drones, you gain a bird's-eye view of your project, offering a new perspective that can inform better decision-making and planning.

Smart home advancements are transforming how we live in barndominiums, making them more comfortable and efficient. AI-driven energy management systems are at the heart of this transformation, optimizing energy use and reducing waste. These systems learn your habits and preferences, adjusting heating, cooling, and lighting to match your lifestyle while conserving resources. The development of intuitive home automation platforms further enhances this experience, allowing you to control various aspects of your home easily. These platforms integrate from security systems to entertainment, providing convenience and peace of mind.

In the realm of design and planning, digital tools are revolutionizing how barndominiums come to life. Virtual reality (VR) offers immersive design visualization, allowing you to explore your future home before a single brick is laid. This technology provides a realistic sense of space and scale, helping you make informed choices about layouts and finishes. You can walk through rooms, assess how light interacts with different areas, and even experiment with different décor styles. Building Information Modeling (BIM) is another powerful tool in the builder's arsenal, streamlining project management from start to finish. BIM creates detailed 3D models encompassing every aspect of the build, from structural components to mechanical systems. This holistic approach ensures that all stakeholders—architects, contractors, and homeowners—are on the same page, reducing errors and enhancing coordination.

However, as with any innovation, there are challenges to consider. Balancing the cost of new technologies with their benefits can be tricky as they often come with a higher price tag. It's crucial to weigh these costs against the long-term savings and advantages they provide. Furthermore, ensuring these technologies are accessible and user-friendly for all homeowners is essential. Not everyone is tech-savvy, and complex systems can be daunting. Ensuring that interfaces are intuitive and support is readily available helps bridge this gap, making technology an ally rather than an obstacle in the barndominium building process.

8.5 BALANCING TRADITION AND INNOVATION IN DESIGN

In the realm of barndominium design, tradition holds a place of reverence. The essence of preserving historical architectural features lies in honoring these elements' authenticity and character. Think of the stately wooden beams that have supported barns for decades, now repurposed to add warmth and rustic charm to a modern home. These features tell a story, one of resilience and timelessness. Incorporating local building practices and materials pays homage to the past and fosters a sense of place and belonging. It connects the home to its surroundings, weaving it into the cultural and historical fabric of the community. This embrace of tradition ensures that barndominiums do not lose sight of their roots while evolving.

Yet, innovation plays an equally vital role in barndominium design, breathing new life into traditional frameworks. The fusion of classic and contemporary styles offers a dynamic approach where the old and new coexist harmoniously. Picture an exterior that retains the weathered patina of aged wood, juxtaposed with sleek, modern lines and large glass panels that invite natural light. This blend creates a visual dialogue between past and contemporary, offering both nostalgia and modernity. Utilizing modern materials enhances durability and efficiency, addressing the demands of today's living while maintaining an aesthetic link to the past. These materials offer superior insulation, energy efficiency, and low maintenance, ensuring that the home is not only beautiful but sustainable.

The synergy between tradition and innovation is where the magic truly happens. Integrating smart technology into rustic settings allows homeowners to enjoy modern conveniences without losing the charm of a bygone era. Imagine controlling your home's lighting and temperature with a smartphone app, all while surrounded by the cozy ambiance of exposed wood and stone. This balance of heritage aesthetics with modern functionality creates comfortable and cutting-edge spaces.

Consider the case of a barndominium that features a classic facade reminiscent of traditional barns yet surprises with a modern interior that rivals contemporary urban lofts. The use of minimalist design elements and open spaces creates an airy, uncluttered feel while retaining the warmth of natural materials. Projects like this showcase how advanced technology can be incorporated without overshadowing traditional charm.

8.6 RECAP: YOUR BARNDOMINIUM JOURNEY AND BEYOND

As we draw our exploration to a close, it's time to reflect on the valuable insights gathered throughout this book. We began by emphasizing the vital role of planning and preparation. These foundational steps are crucial in crafting a barndominium that meets your needs and exceeds them. By understanding the intricacies of zoning laws and budgeting, you lay the groundwork for a successful build. We delved deep into the importance of customization, allowing you to create a space that truly reflects your personality and lifestyle. The focus on sustainability underscored our commitment to eco-friendly living, encouraging the use of renewable resources and energy-efficient systems that benefit not only you but also the planet.

Reflecting on your personal progress is an integral part of this process. Take a moment to assess how your goals and expectations have evolved since you first considered building a barndominium. Perhaps your initial vision has transformed, adapting to new ideas or constraints. This evolution is a testament to your growth and learning.

Recognize the skills you've acquired along the way, from understanding building codes to making informed design choices. Each step and each decision contributes to your overall journey and shapes you into a more knowledgeable and confident homeowner. Celebrate these achievements, no matter how small, as they form the foundation of your success.

Looking ahead, continue to engage with the barndominium community for support and inspiration. Staying informed about industry trends and innovations is key to ensuring your home remains relevant and efficient. The world of barndominiums is ever-evolving, with new technologies and design philosophies emerging regularly. Networking with other homeowners and professionals provides fresh perspectives and ideas that can enhance your living experience. Whether it's attending workshops, joining online forums, or participating in local meetups, these interactions enrich your understanding and open doors to new possibilities.

Encourage yourself to keep exploring and expanding your horizons. Experiment with new design ideas or technologies to enhance your barndominium's functionality and aesthetic appeal. Consider future expansions or modifications that might better suit your changing lifestyle. Perhaps you envision adding a workshop, a guest suite, or even integrating smart home technologies for increased convenience. These possibilities allow your home to grow with you, adapting to your needs as they evolve. Embrace these opportunities for innovation, knowing that your barndominium is a dynamic space capable of continuous transformation.

Remember that building a barndominium is not just about creating a physical structure but crafting a living environment that nurtures and inspires. As you move forward, let the insights and experiences gained here guide you. Your barndominium is more than a home; it's a reflection of your vision and values, a testament to what you can achieve with dedication and creativity. Keep pushing boundaries, exploring new avenues, and celebrating the journey. This is just the beginning of a life enriched by the possibilities your barndominium offers.

BE A BARNDOMINIUM INSPIRATION!

I'm excited for the future ahead of you, and I urge you to turn your barndominium dream into a reality. But before you go, why not take a moment to inspire someone else to follow their own lifestyle dreams?

Simply by sharing your honest opinion of this book and a little about your own barndominium journey, you'll show new readers exactly where they can find all the guidance they need to get their idea off the ground.

LEAVE A REVIEW!

Thank you so much for your support. I'm excited for the home you're going to create.

Scan the QR code below

CONCLUSION

As you reach the end of this journey through "Barndominium Building and Living: The Beginners Guide to Building and Living in a Barndominium," let's take a moment to reflect on the path we've traveled together. Each chapter has been crafted to provide you with insights and practical guidance, empowering you to embark on the exciting adventure of creating your own barndominium.

We began with an exploration of what a barndominium is, delving into its unique balance of rustic charm and modern functionality. We examined the benefits that make these homes appealing, from affordability and flexibility to the lifestyle shift they encourage. You learned about the potential for customization, the integration of sustainable building practices, and how to debunk common myths associated with barndominiums.

Planning was a major focus, and we discussed creating a vision for your home, budgeting effectively, and selecting the right location. We also emphasized the importance of thoughtful design, balancing aesthetics with functionality, and navigating zoning laws. Moving into the construction phase, we covered building codes, securing permits, and overcoming bureaucratic challenges. You gained insights into selecting and managing a team, balancing DIY efforts with professional help, and ensuring quality workmanship.

Designing and decorating your barndominium becomes a creative endeavor as your project takes shape. We explored intermingling rustic and modern aesthetics, maximizing space with open-concept living, and the potential of loft designs. Personalization through decor and integrating smart home technologies and sustainable choices for a greener home were highlighted.

Transitioning to life in a barndominium involves embracing minimalism, building community connections, and considering self-sufficient living. Maintenance tips ensure your home remains in top condition, and planning for future expansion keeps your options open. Real-life success stories and emerging trends offered inspiration and a glimpse into the future of barndominium living.

Throughout this book, I hope I've reinforced the vision of guiding you, a barndominium beginner, through this transformative process. Each chapter was designed to address both the technical and emotional aspects of building and living in a barndominium. The key takeaways include effective planning and budgeting, the joy of customization, and the emotional journey of adapting to a new lifestyle.

Reflect on your own emotional journey. You started with curiosity and have now gained a wealth of knowledge to make informed decisions. Acknowledge the adjustments you may need to make, both psychologically and emotionally, as you transition into this new way of living.

Please take a moment to reflect on how the information and ideas shared can be applied to your unique circumstances and goals. Consider what aspects of this journey resonate with you and how you can integrate them into your own life. Each step you take brings you closer to realizing your dream.

As you stand on the brink of action, feel inspired to take the necessary steps towards building your barndominium. Use the knowledge and resources in this book to confidently navigate your journey. Whether you're just starting to plan or are already immersed in the process, remember the potential rewards and personal growth that lie ahead.

Your involvement with the barndominium community can provide ongoing support and inspiration. Engage with others who share your passion, and utilize resources to stay informed and motivated. This community is a valuable network that can enhance your experience and offer encouragement along the way.

Stay curious and open to exploration. New trends, technologies, and design ideas are constantly emerging. Embrace these opportunities to adapt your home and lifestyle, ensuring your barndominium remains a reflection of your evolving needs and desires.

On a personal note, it's been my passion to help you achieve your dream lifestyle in a barndominium. I hope this book serves as a trusted companion on your journey. May your path be filled with success and satisfaction as you create a home that truly reflects who you are. Thank you for allowing me to be part of your barndominium adventure. I'm excited to see where your journey takes you.

REFERENCES

History of Barndominium - How Barns Develop Into Houses https://www.tallboxdesign.com/what-is-a-barndominium/

The Pros and Cons of Steel Framing vs Wood Framing https://tampasteel.com/pros-and-cons-of-steel-vs-wood-home-framing/

Building a Sustainable Barndominium | Tristate Buildings LLC https://www.tristatebuildings.com/blog/sustainable-barndominium

Barndominium Interior Designs & Ideas https://www.salterspiralstair.com/blog/unique-barndominium-designs/?srsltid=AfmBOooKl7orMP1AfDtX5bRIoMosj4OP5nqXNxfRs-Qt2vBiLpir_P7u

New Trends in Barndominium Design for 2024 and Beyond https://buildmax.com/new-trends-in-barndominium-design-for-2024-and-beyond/?srsltid=AfmBOoqMoapCoXpBwLK4dNNqfODuZorp1qK6uBKCoPWwkR7ZoWOH_eup

Average cost to build a barndominium - Detail Guide https://www.constructelements.com/post/average-cost-to-build-a-barndominium

Know the Codes for Barndominiums https://fabral.com/know-the-codes-for-barndominiums-when-and-where-can-you-build/

Tips for Designing Multi-Functional Spaces in Your Home https://www.hammerschmidtinc.com/tips-for-designing-multi-functional-spaces-in-your-home/

Navigating Building Codes and Regulations for ... https://alldraft.com/navigating-building-codes-and-regulations-for-barndominiums-a-comprehensive-guide/

The Ultimate Guide to Building Permits in Texas for Owner ... https://www.builtgreentexas.com/the-ultimate-guide-to-building-permits/

Avoiding Common Pitfalls in Building Permit Compliance https://www.archistar.ai/blog/avoiding-common-pitfalls-in-building-permit-compliance/

Why does the US have varying building codes and ... https://www.quora.com/Why-does-the-US-have-varying-building-codes-and-ordinances-in-different-towns-and-cities-Is-there-a-national-standard-for-these-regulations

How to Find and Vet Home Contractors https://centeredbydesign.com/how-to-find-and-vet-home-contractors/

Great Tips for Building a Barndominium on a Budget https://buildmax.com/great-tips-for-building-a-barndominium-on-a-budget/

Five Essential Elements of a Construction Contract https://www.cotneycl.com/five-essential-elements-of-a-construction-contract/

REFERENCES

Why Effective Communication is Vital in Construction Projects https://www.outbuild.com/blog/why-is-communication-important-in-construction

7 Steps and Best Practices in Construction Site Preparation https://perlo.biz/7-steps-and-best-practices-in-construction-site-preparation/

Barndominium Framing Options https://avobarndominiums.com/barndominium-framing-options/

Energy-Efficient Roofing: A Homeowners Guide (2024) https://www.ecowatch.com/roofing/roof-energy-efficiency

The Impact of Weather on Your Project https://www.catrentalstore.com/en_US/blog/impact-of-weather.html

What is Rustic Chic Décor? https://chesmar.com/what-is-rustic-chic-decor/

75 Open Concept Living Room Ideas You'll Love https://www.houzz.com/photos/open-concept-living-room-ideas-phbr1-bp~t_718~a_63-500

Best Smart Home Devices of 2024 https://www.cnet.com/home/smart-home/best-smart-home-devices/

Eco-Friendly and Chic: Sustainable Interior Design Trends ... https://tanic.design/blog/sustainable-interior-design-trends

How to Maximize Small Spaces: 10 Design Tips ... https://www.newthresholds.com/how-to-maximize-small-spaces-10-design-tips-and-tricks/

Rural Community Building Best Practices https://wvhub.org/6-best-practices-for-rural-community-development/

How to live off the grid: the ultimate guide for beginners ... https://ecoshack.com/how-to-live-off-the-grid/

Barndominium Maintenance: How to Keep Your Barndo in ... https://barndominiumsintexas.com/barndominium-maintenance-how-to-keep-your-barndo-in-top-shape/

From Barn to Barndominium: Inspiring Success Stories of ... https://www.jlbarndominiumartists.com/from-barn-to-barndominium-inspiring-success-stories-of-transformation/

New Trends in Barndominium Design for 2024 and Beyond https://buildmax.com/new-trends-in-barndominium-design-for-2024-and-beyond/

Building a Sustainable Barndominium | Tristate Buildings LLC https://www.tristatebuildings.com/blog/sustainable-barndominium

Building a Sustainable Barndominium | Tristate Buildings LLC https://www.tristatebuildings.com/blog/sustainable-barndominium

Prihandito, Bayu. November 18, 2023. "96 Never Too Late Quotes: Turn Your Dreams into Reality." Life Architekture. Accessed January 6, 2025. https://lifearchitekture.com/blogs/quotes-affirmations/never-too-late-quotes.